T0328655

Cambridge Elements

Elements in Contentious Politics
edited by
David S. Meyer
University of California, Irvine
Suzanne Staggenborg
University of Pittsburgh

CONTENTIOUS POLITICS IN EMERGENCY CRITICAL JUNCTURES

Progressive Social Movements during the Pandemic

Donatella della Porta
Scuola Normale Superiore, Florence

CAMBRIDGE
UNIVERSITY PRESS

CAMBRIDGE
UNIVERSITY PRESS

University Printing House, Cambridge CB2 8BS, United Kingdom

One Liberty Plaza, 20th Floor, New York, NY 10006, USA

477 Williamstown Road, Port Melbourne, VIC 3207, Australia

314–321, 3rd Floor, Plot 3, Splendor Forum, Jasola District Centre,
New Delhi – 110025, India

103 Penang Road, #05–06/07, Visioncrest Commercial, Singapore 238467

Cambridge University Press is part of the University of Cambridge.

It furthers the University's mission by disseminating knowledge in the pursuit of
education, learning, and research at the highest international levels of excellence.

www.cambridge.org
Information on this title: www.cambridge.org/9781009016483
DOI: 10.1017/9781009025638

© Donatella della Porta 2022

First published 2022

A catalogue record for this publication is available from the British Library.

ISBN 978-1-009-01648-3 Paperback
ISSN 2633-3570 (online)
ISSN 2633-3562 (print)

Contentious Politics In Emergency Critical Junctures

Progressive Social Movements during the Pandemic

Elements in Contentious Politics

DOI: 10.1017/9781009025638
First published online: July 2022

Donatella della Porta
Scuola Normale Superiore, Florence

Author for correspondence: Donatella della Porta, Donatella.dellapor
ta@sns.it

Abstract: Social movements have often played an important role in emergencies, mobilizing in defence of those rights that they perceive as being at risk or more urgently needed than ever. In general, progressive social movements develop in moments of intense change, mobilizing with the aim of turning them to their advantage. The specific balance of challenges and opportunities faced by progressive social movements during the Covid-19 crisis is a central question addressed in this Element. Based on existing research on the first phases of the Covid-19 pandemic, this Element addresses the ways in which the health emergency had an impact on the repertoire of action, organizational networks and collective framing of progressive social movements that adapted to the pandemic conditions and the related crises, but also tried to transform them.

Keywords: social movements, contentious politics, pandemic, Covid-19, progressive politics

ISBNs: 9781009016483 (PB), 9781009025638 (OC)
ISSNs: 2633-3570 (online), 2633-3562 (print)

Contents

1 Progressive Social Movements during the Pandemic: An Introduction

Social Movements and Covid-19: An Introduction

With the declaration of a global pandemic in March 2020 and the subsequent imposition of lockdown regulations, the immediate expectation was that social movements were destined to enter into a period of latency, or at the very least, invisibility. Given the introduction of severe restrictions on the use of public space, it seemed that Covid-19 had managed to halt the incredibly intense period of global protest that had shaken the world in the autumn of 2019, with peaks of contestation in places as diverse as Lebanon, Chile, Hong Kong and Catalonia. In reality, however, the pandemic period proved to be extremely rich in terms of contentious politics. It was during this period that in Chile, for example, citizens voted to change the Pinochet-era constitution and developed a participatory constitutional process, while protests also continued in Hong Kong, Lebanon and Catalonia (Chan and Tsui 2020; Kassir 2020), albeit in somewhat weakened forms.

Not only did the global wave of protests not come to an end with the emergency, but the health crisis triggered an intense period of contestation, during which activists and organizations from pre-existing progressive social movements remobilized and others emerged around issues such as social rights, labour rights, gender rights and environmental rights, often combining their causes with calls for global health rights. As Sutapa Chattopadhyay, Lesley Wood and Laurence Cox (2020, 1) outlined in their introduction to a special issue of the journal *Interface* devoted to protest during the pandemic, '[t]he world is on fire, with both fever and flame. After a few months of lockdown, things are erupting in new ways. ... Around the world, movements are strategizing about how to ensure that no one is left behind.' By looking at these social movements, in what follows I will reflect on the opportunities and challenges that the pandemic presents for progressive movements and, more broadly, for progressive politics.

Although the pandemic has not stalled progressive movements, one might, however, expect it to have transformed them, challenging them to adapt to new conditions and pushing them to develop alternative practices and ideas in order to address the emergency. While the pandemic encompasses a long period – that has still to come to an end – in this Element I will focus on two main phases in its evolution: the lockdown phase, between March and June 2020, and the initial reopening, from July to December of the same year. In order to understand this surge in protests, the concepts and hypotheses developed in social movement studies prove extremely useful. Their repertoires of action, organizational structures and collective framing can undoubtedly be linked to both emerging grievances and broad opportunities and constraints. In addition, research on pre–Covid-19 social movements provides very useful insights for the analysis of the most recent waves of contentious politics, as deeply rooted movement networks and cultures have undoubtedly affected the strategic choices of the various actors converging in mobilizations, showing continuities in terms of organizational structures and repertoires of actions.

As with every intense period of contention, one might nevertheless expect transformation to occur, as social movement organizations, disruptive collective actions and calls for social change spread and new conflicts emerge. Moreover, while much research on social movements has addressed normal, predictable periods, it would seem that theories of social movements require updating in order to understand contentious mobilization in exceptional periods such as the pandemic. There are a number of reasons why this could be beneficial. First and foremost, given that it is an abnormal event, the pandemic challenges the assumptions of predictability, stability and structuration on which so much theorization in social and political sciences is based. As a juncture that is both global in its scale and critical in its nature, the spread of Covid-19 has somewhat weakened the power of existing structures, triggering an 'eventful temporality' (Sewell 1996) that challenges routines and increases the importance of agency. Given the high degree of uncertainty, movement choices cannot be built on solid routines, but rather must be taken in the heat of the moment and in the face of unfamiliar circumstances. While pre-existing resources and opportunities are undoubtedly relevant for mobilization, they would appear to have been weakened by the pandemic. This in turn has disrupted existing networks and produced new threats, rendering a number of previously common practices and ideas unsuited to facing challenges that have emerged.

As will be argued in what follows, analyses of contentious politics in such uncertain times can be especially stimulating for theorization on social movements. Indeed, given the fact that social movements set out to challenge authority, we can assume that new codes (Melucci 1996) and emerging norms (Turner 1996) acquire all the more relevance in what Mark Beissinger (2002) has defined as intense times, in contrast to the quiet, predictable, routine periods that social scientists are accustomed to analyzing. While aggrieved citizens do not automatically rebel, moments of high disruption of the quotidian, such as economic crises or wars, have been proven to exacerbate discontent, and with it to increase the potential for the intensification of contentious politics (Tarrow 2015; della Porta 2017). During these intense periods, mobilization is facilitated by available opportunities and resources, but threats and perceived urgencies can also generate reactions in the form of collective action (della Porta 2020a). Critical moments tend to augment the relevance of collective agency. This is due to the fact that, given the crisis of the existing institutions, emergent actors, such as social movements, can play an extremely relevant role in the construction of new norms and the experimentation of new practices.

While a pandemic is a rare event, studies on social movements have occasionally addressed periods of emergency that, in addition to other health crises, have included natural disasters, deep economic recessions and wars. Research on these classes of events has signalled that although emergencies present particular challenges, they also provide opportunities for contentious politics, deeply impacting on their forms. Their development has partly been linked to the nature of the emergency itself, and partly to the (local/national/ global) political and social contexts in which it happens (Aber, Rossi and von Bulow 2021). While structural constraints are present, periods of emergency are rather unstructured and unpredictable and particularly sensitive to the impact of contingent events (Schmitter and O'Donnel 1986; Beissinger 2002 della Porta 2017).

As several studies have indicated, during these intense periods, progressive social movements must face challenges such as:

- the drastic increase in the material needs of a growing part of the population,
- the scapegoating of marginal groups,
- the shrinking of physical space for collective action,
- the centralization of power in the executive branch,
- increasing censorship,
- the frequent deployment of the military.

Faced with such intense pressure, social movement organizations may disband or be forced to invest all of their energy on the immediate survival of their constituency, with little time for long-term strategizing.

However, on the other hand, there are also opportunities for protest, as emergencies enhance conflicts over scarce and direly needed resources that often find their expression in collective action. Faced with the disruption of everyday life, forms of collective action that emerge to deal with immediate needs may bring about politicized claims and practices of self-empowerment. In action, as old social movement organizations encounter new groups that are formed to address a specific emergency, the shared risks might promote alliances and fuel solidarity. It is especially when sacrifices are demanded that claims for citizens' rights tend to spread. The perception that previous arrangements have failed paves the way in the search for alternatives, while ties of solidarity can be fostered by innovation and heated emotions.

The Covid-19 pandemic can be considered to be a particular type of critical moment, as it is driven by a sudden and dramatic emergency that has deeply affected contentious politics. Although lockdown policies, which were established to control the spread of the contagion, initially constrained collective action in the street, contentious politics spread very quickly with various forms of mobilizations addressing the many serious crises that accompanied the spread of the virus. It is particularly noticeable that although the mass media has mainly focussed on anti-lockdown protests, often orchestrated by radical right-wing groups and virus-deniers, within progressive movements there was a rise in protests on issues such as housing, income and education, as well as on demands for participation and against repression. From initial reports and preliminary studies, these protests appear to have been built on previous global waves of contention – from the global justice movement to anti-austerity mobilizations – as well as on the experiences of resistance in different countries to a backlash from right-wing movements and governments (Meyer and Tarrow 2019; della Porta 2020b).

However, these protests also present a number of new characteristics, which may be connected to the sudden rupture produced by the pandemic. While many anti-lockdown protests were very visible, my analysis is instead primarily concerned with the actions of what we might call progressive social movements. Although progress is a contested term (Allen 2016; della Porta 2020), I use it here to define actors that struggle for an inclusive vision of a just society and for a deepening of democracy. Progress is thus understood as aiming for

> the liberation (or 'emancipation') of collectivities (for example: citizens, classes, nations, minorities, income categories, even mankind), be it the liberation from want, ignorance, exploitative relations, or the freedom of such collectives to govern themselves autonomously, that is, without being dependent on or controlled by others. Furthermore, the freedom that results from liberation applies equally to all, with equality serving as a criterion to ensure that liberation does not in fact become a mere privilege of particular social categories.' (Offe 2011, 79–80)

In this sense, progressive social movements are those that combine attention to social justice with positive freedom (della Porta and Rucht 1995). The analysis will deal with protests that present claims for broader inclusion of citizens (Ypi 2012).

The specific balance of challenges and opportunities faced by progressive social movements during the Covid-19 crisis is a central question addressed in this Element. Even if research is still at an early stage – and many observations outlined in what follows must therefore be considered as tentative – there are, nonetheless, a multiplicity of reports and initial analyses that make it possible (and useful) to develop some empirically based reflections on this dramatic period. While time is required to carry out an in-depth assessment of the development and eventual outcomes of these mobilizations within systematic cross-national comparative perspectives, some of their common trends are already visible:

- First and foremost, progressive movements have built upon a complex repertoire of contention, including disruptive protests, as well as forms of mutual help and alternative knowledge building.
- Secondly, these activities have been fuelled not only by existing social movement organizations, but also by newly emerging groups and networks.
- Thirdly, contentious politics has bridged new concerns relating to the health emergency with a core discourse on social justice and civil rights. Activists have pointed to the need to develop social rights, as the pandemic has made the effects of social inequalities, as well as gender, generational and ethnic inequalities, all the more visible and all the more unacceptable. In denouncing declining institutional accountability and in some cases even repression, progressive movements have combined calls for public health and welfare policies with appeals for greater citizen participation.

Against all the odds, the initial stages in the timeline of the Covid-19 pandemic have been marked by what media and activists have already termed a new global wave of protest. Both the fear of contagion and lock-down measures seemed heavily poised to jeopardize collective action. Activists have, however, invented new forms of contention with which to not only express their increasing grievances, but also to spread ideas for change. Focussing on social movements that endeavour to expand social rights and political participation, this Element aims to contribute to the reflection on how the pandemic affects progressive politics in general. While recognizing the fact that the specific impact of the virus has been broadly different in different parts of the world, the Element aims especially at singling out a number of global trends.

The reminder of this section will conceptualize the pandemic period as rooted in extraordinary circumstances, pointing to some expectations related to the dynamics of progressive social movements in such intense moments. Following on from this, and on the basis of initial empirical evidence that can be gleaned from documents and reports on protests covering the twelve months between March 2020 and February 2021, the Element will identify some of the main interpretative lines of contentious politics in emergent critical junctures, look-ing at forms of contention, collective framing and organizational repertoires. While most of the case studies refer to Europe and North America, an attempt has also been made to cover cases in the Global South (albeit less systematically). As it is too early to empirically test any hypotheses, use will be made of existing evidence in order to illustrate the plausibility of some of the interpretations put forward on the democratic role played by progressive social movements during the Covid-19 crisis. In examining the mobilization of these groups on social rights and civil liberties, but also the challenges that are still to be addressed, I aim at developing hypotheses rather than proving them (della Porta 2008) while reflecting on specific characteristics of repertoires of action (Section 2), organizational processes (Section 3) and collective framing (Section 4) in an intense period marked by the pandemic crisis. The conclusion (Section 5) will summarize the challenges and perspectives for progressive social movements in the Covid-19 era, suggesting avenues for future research.

Pandemics as Emergency Junctures

The Covid-19 crisis can be defined as an *emergency critical juncture*, characterized by a sudden rupture produced by a catastrophic event, that has an impact on the whole world and is triggered by an airborne, highly contagious virus, which quickly developed into economic, social and political crises. In general, social movements can trigger, or at least adapt to, what neo-institutionalists call critical junctures. These are defined as '(1) a major episode of institutional innovation, (2) occurring in distinct ways, (3) and generating an enduring legacy' (Collier and Munck 2017, 2). In contrast to normal periods, critical junctures are periods of 'crisis or strain that existing policies and institutions are ill-suited to resolve' (Roberts 2015, 65).

As in other intense moments in history, progressive social movements might be expected to play an important role during a pandemic, mobilizing for an expansion of civic, political and social rights (Marshall 1992). Given that the expansion of rights is neither a consolidated trend, nor does it proceed at the same pace for different social, gender, generational and ethnic groups (della Porta 2017), progressive social movements have constantly mobilized to defend and extend such rights. This can be seen to have taken place in recent decades, which have been characterized by increasing inequalities and declining democratic qualities (Morlino 2012; Therborn 2013). A crisis such as the Covid-19 pandemic can, therefore, be expected to fuel old conflicts and create new ones.

Social rights and democratic qualities are of the utmost importance during emergency periods, which require a careful assessment of the trade-off between different rights and liberties. As Baldwin (2005, 247) noted in a comparative analysis of health policies during the AIDS pandemic, 'attempts to curtail epidemics raise – in the guise of public health – the most enduring political dilemma: how to reconcile the individual's claim to autonomy and liberty with the community's concern with safety . . . . How are individual rights and the public good pursued simultaneously?' We can add here that exceptional circumstances, such as global pandemics, create dilemmas not only between individual liberties and public security, but also between health protection and other social rights, since lockdown measures halt or dramatically reduce access to social or educational public services as well as other services such as public transport.

During the Covid-19 crisis these dilemmas have been apparent as states of emergency have been called in different forms by different countries. Indeed, the pandemic has been considered

> a social and economic shock as well as a political crisis and a psychological trauma. There was an abrupt end to mobility as, one by one, states imposed lockdowns and quarantines with the result that normal life ceased. . . . What at first seemed possible only in a dictatorship became an increasingly accepted way to respond to the danger posed by the coronavirus. (Delanty 2021, 1)

While states of emergency have at different times been contemplated in democratic regimes in order to address various types of disasters, there is no doubt that they affect political opportunities for social movements, reducing the checks and balances on institutions as well as the capacity of citizens to hold their governments accountable. Indeed, in democracies there is a need to justify the use of a state of emergency, which is usually done by claiming that the measures taken are extraordinary, enacted in response to necessity and a lack of alternatives, thus masking the presence of very significant political choices. As Jonathan White has noted, in relation to the financial crisis in Europe in the 2010s,

> [e]mergency rule is conducted and narrated as the encounter with unfamiliar situations that demand to be handled on their own terms. It is about doing things differently because the situation at hand is different. At least in terms of its own rationale, but also in view of the creations it gives rise to, emergency rule is geared to the singularity of a certain moment. (White 2020, 188)

Paradoxically, '[w]hile emergency rule entails frenetic decision making, its decisions are rationalized as unchosen and unavoidable in substance and timing' (White 2021, 85).

As governance in emergencies tends to be informal and unaccountable, exceptional powers break with procedural rules, with the suspension of some rights and a centralization of decision-making in the national government. Given that the most important decisions are taken in haste, emergencies also increase discretion, due to a lack of clarity about the limits and the implications of the decisions taken (White 2021, 81). As Sheppele (2010) has synthetized, emergency scripts involve elements such as executive centralization, with a decline in the power of the parliament; militarization, with the military positioned as key respondent to the threat; procedural shortcuts, as procedural checks are bypassed; ban on demonstrations, with the restrictions on freedom of movement; constraints on freedom of speech, with censorship and criminalization; and decreasing transparency, with governmental action blanketed in secrecy as well as increasing surveillance up to and including anticipatory violence against opponents.

In the case of the Covid-19 pandemic, attempts have been made to address the crisis through emergency measures that have dramatically constrained rights of movement, assembly and expatriation. While this has happened to different degrees in different regimes – with more drastic and arbitrary constraints in authoritarian regimes – the very presence of an emergency has undoubtedly affected the functioning of public institutions at all territorial levels and worldwide. Under these circumstances, contentious politics seem all the more relevant, albeit its development is also all the more constrained.

A further aspect that has been highlighted by the Covid-19 crisis is the fact that emergencies not only affect civil rights, but also social rights, as they magnify the effects of the unequal distribution of resources within and across countries. Social protection is especially at stake as living conditions related to core social rights (such as health, work, housing and education) are jeopardized by exceptional circumstances. As is the case during war, catastrophes or deep economic depressions, the disruption of everyday life hits some sections of the population especially hard, increasing class, gender, generational and ethnic inequalities. While a disruption of everyday life has been a common experience worldwide during the pandemic, the degree of suffering has been unquestionably influenced by pre-existing conditions in terms of social rights. The pandemic has highlighted the lethal consequences of differential access to public healthcare, all the more so in countries that have historically had a weak welfare state (such as the United States, but even more dramatically in the Global South), or countries where neoliberal policies enacted by right-wing governments have been more widespread (as in the United Kingdom). Even countries that had once been considered to be endowed with generous welfare provisions (i.e. in Europe) have also seen the negative long-term consequences of the commodification of health services, cuts to resources for public institutions, and reductions to the number of health workers and their salaries. These have all been pointed to as increasing the spread and lethality of the virus. Thus, the coronavirus crisis revealed the 'weakness of state capacity – underfunded, part-privatized and underprepared health systems' (White 2021, 77). As a result, while the Covid-19 pandemic was initially presented as having a levelling effect, 'as the pathogen infects human beings indiscriminately of social status and the containment measures disrupted the economic engines of whole national economies, the public health crisis in fact laid bare existing inequalities and deepened them farther' (Azmanova 2021, 244). The importance of concerns for climate change and the urgency with which they need to be addressed has also been highlighted by the fact that it was in the most polluted areas that the contagion was particularly intense and mortality highest. Aside from the increase in episodes of violence against women, the pandemic also made blatantly clear both the importance of care activities and their unequal gender distribution, with women bearing the heaviest burden in this regard.

While an in-depth cross-country comparative analysis of these challenges will require time to be developed, the weakness of the welfare state and the lack or decline of democratic rights seem to have increased social discrimination and the repression of civil and political rights. Trump's United States, Bolsonaro's Brazil and Modi's India are the main illustrations of countries in which weak welfare states and high levels of repression have fuelled the spread of the virus with the most deadly effects. From an historical perspective, general trends that have aggravated the effects of the virus include a reduced capacity for state intervention in social protection as well as a general backlash against the previous achievements of progressive social movements.

Progressive Social Movements in Emergency Periods

Social movements have often played an important role in emergencies, mobilizing in defence of those rights that they perceive as being at risk or more urgently needed than ever. In general, progressive social movements develop in moments of intense change, mobilizing with the aim of turning them to their advantage. As opportunities and resources are not just static givens but rather emerge from relational dynamics in intense periods, social movements can become important catalysts for change, contributing to the emergence of new norms during periods in which 'usual conventions cease to guide social action and people collectively transcend, bypass or subvert established institutional patterns and structures' (Turner and Killian 1987, 3; see also Turner 1996).

In social movement studies, attention has turned anew to the role of social movements in exceptional periods, as opposed to normal periods. In periods of crisis and rapid transformation, 'the accepted norms of behaviour, the ones that guide behaviours in everyday, institutionalized, normal, quotidian activities, don't apply because of unusual or atypical social contexts: a catastrophe, a suddenly imposed grievance, a moral shock, a disaster. Social actors turn to each other to make sense of the situation, not to some objective and compelling character of reality' (Johnston 2018, 8). Thus, critical events, such as disasters, alter both the environmental conditions and our perceptions of them, increasing the potential for coalition but also for division. However, their role as precipitating factors or turning points is, in fact, mediated by existing social movement organizations (Staggenborg 1993), as well as by new movement organizations.

Even before the onset of the current pandemic, the recent past had been defined as a momentous period: the terms 'the Great Transformation', 'the Great Recession' as well as 'the Great Regression' have frequently been used as shorthands to define the period following the financial breakdown of 2008 that triggered the sizeable mobilization of so-called movements of the crises (della Porta 2015; della Porta and Mattoni 2014). In this context, researchers have increasingly addressed protests as transformative events (della Porta 2020a). Moments of rupture are thus recognized as incredibly important in defining new paths for progressive change (della Porta 2017). Indeed, eventful protests are 'contentious and potentially subversive practices that challenge normalized practices, modes of causation, or system of authority' (Beissinger 2002, 14).

In general, extraordinary challenges have 'profound effects on the structuring of strategic action fields across society' as 'crises undermine all kinds of linkages in society and make it difficult for groups to reproduce their power'. At the same time, dramatic crises prompt the 'attribution of new opportunities and threats leading to the appropriation or creation of new organizational vehicles for the purpose of engaging in innovative, contentious interaction with other field actors' (Fligstein and McAdam 2012, 101). A relevant example of an area in which a great deal of research has been carried out on critical junctures is in relation to war. As 'states make war but war makes states' (Tilly 1975, 42), political contention has been implicated in the dynamics of war from the onset. This is seen, for example, in advance of a war, with mobilizations for or against war; during a war, in support of or in resistance to the war effort; and in the wake of a war, with the opening up of political opportunities to change state politics and even overturn regimes (Tarrow 2015, 15).

Therefore, moments of crisis often intensify calls for rights by disrupting the quotidian and triggering discontent, but also by creating the expectation that sacrifices have to be compensated by tangible recognition of belonging to a community of destiny (Tilly 1992, 10). Research has, in fact, noted that contention tends to grow during wars: 'as states impose higher taxes, armies suffer defeats, and the body bags return from the front, enthusiasm for war dampens. Movements develop in reaction to these costs but also against the constriction of rights that almost always occurs when states go to war'

(Tarrow 2015, 24). In the wake of the war, rights can be enhanced, so much so that 'many of the reforms we take for granted today – the citizen army, women's suffrage, and the welfare state – were spurred by war, preparation of war, and contention in war's wake' (Tarrow 2015, 28; see also Starr 2010). As several studies have indicated, the specific balance of threats and opportunities that emerge for contentious politics in extraordinary periods varies, however, as it is influenced by the general social and political conditions that preceded it. In the case of wars, democratic developments and the state of contentious politics in the pre-war period, the extent to which different sectors of the population are affected by the war, the ways in which the war is concluded and the presence of political allies within a state's borders all play a role in the post-war developments of civil, political and social rights.

Although pandemics and wars are different types of crisis events, they do display some similarities. In both cases major disruptions are created in everyday life, with governments imposing various forms of constraints on freedom and, at the same time, often unable (or unwilling) to address the social inequalities that are exacerbated by the crisis. In contrast to a war, the current pandemic is characterized by its sudden outbreak. However, it has lasted for a long enough period to trigger a great deal of contentious politics, which in some cases has proven successful in defending citizenship rights.

The Contentious Construction of a Health Crisis

Emergency critical junctures are influenced by the specific characteristics of the exceptional circumstances that triggered the crisis as they are filtered through a social construction (Quarantelli and Dynes 1977; Tierny 2019). As the narrative of an emergency develops during the events, social movements have the potential to influence the perceptions of its causes and consequences (Kreuder-Sonne 2019). Although the disruption of everyday life triggers frustration and outrage, the development of a collective response is heavily affected by the ways in which a problem (in this case a crisis) is framed (Rao and Greve Insead 2018). The politicization of the diagnostic and prognostic frames can stimulate protests especially when the event is considered not to be a natural catastrophe but rather a man-made one.

Research on health crises has indicated that contagious diseases are particularly likely to spread suspicion among members of the community, thus reducing resilience. While attribution of personal similarity to the victims can increase compassion, when similarity is denied, victims are more easily blamed. In general, 'contagious diseases outbreaks lead to blaming either the infected or another social group as culprit' (Rao and Greve Insead 2018, 8), with a frequent spread of rumours and the triggering of moral panics. As a matter of fact, the higher the mortality rate of a contagious disease, the higher the chance that others are feared and scapegoated, while it is also more likely it is that interpersonal trust breaks down (Rao and Greve Insead 2018). Airborne infectious diseases have especially highlighted the fragility of individuals and collectives (Delanty 2021). Indeed, historical analyses have pointed to the impact of plagues on societal evolution (Turner 2021), stressing the capacity of microscopic viruses to trigger macroscopical changes (McNeill 1998; Snowden 2020). Other studies have also shown how the cognitive assessment of various health crises influenced their effects (Rosenberg 1989), as plagues have prompted the search for meaningful (religious or secular) interpretations (Turner 2021). In the case of the AIDS global epidemic, which has killed 35 million people since 1981, it was its framing as a 'gay disease' that constituted one of the fundamental conditions for the mobilization for gay rights (Kleres 2018; Epstein 1996).

It is undoubtable that the social construction of diseases is influenced by general and country-specific evolutions in the visions of health. Historically speaking there has been a shift in how contagion has been conceived and the approach taken to tackling the problem. During the Middle Ages, there was a conception of contagion as being caused by infectious agents, with quarantine employed as a remedy. In the nineteenth century, illnesses were attributed to unhealthy environments and sanitation became the main method to tackle their spread. The current conceptions of illness point to personal dispositions, with appeals to discourage unhealthy habits and encourage healthy ones. The modern conception of public health 'entailed an individualization of public health as the new scientific knowledge made individual hygiene focal. The latter involved abandoning coercive means of quarantinism in favour of strategies of mass persuasion and education – health education, promotion of domestic hygiene, etc.' (Kleres 2018, 25). Adding weight to the significance of individual behaviour and personal responsibility, medical knowledge has attributed obesity, heart diseases or certain cancers to poor diet, tobacco use, alcohol consumption, insufficient physical exercise, etc. Increasingly, voluntary changes in individual behaviour became central to public health as 'what appeared to be a loosening of (coercive) social controls in fact relied on their internationalization by moralizing health' (Kleres 2018, 27–8). Thus, a democratic ethos of good citizens included desirable health behaviour as 'sneezing and suffrage were linked' (Baldwin 2005, 15), denying the impact of the social context in the spread of diseases. In fact, '[i]ndividual behavior was the concern: overeating, overworking, overdrinking, undexercizing, overcopulating' (16). As noted in the social construction of mental illness (Crossley 2006), epidemiological develop-ments strengthened this individualization, which has also been a dominant factor in approaches to the Covid-19 pandemic. Against this vision of individual responsibility, progressive social movements have pointed to collective responsibility, singling out contextual conditions linked to inter-sectional inequalities as having deadly effects, stigmatizing the neoliberal order for the cuts in public health as well as the many inequalities that have increased the cost of the pandemic in terms of lives lost.

While the current crisis has seen a return to quarantine and sanitation measures, the debates surrounding the pandemic have also been characterized by a re-emergence of the concept of individual responsibility, particularly in relation to the higher risk posed by the disease to overweight individuals, those who travel frequently and those younger sections of society that pay less attention to public health regulations. During the Covid-19 pandemic, as in other emergencies, a fundamental task for progressive social movements is the construction of a narrative that makes it possible to single out human-made causes, shared destinies and political solutions. However, once again, the outcomes of health crises are not pre-determined. Rather, they are influenced by social and political struggles that take place over their very meaning, and the solutions to them. At the end of World War I, the Spanish Flu, together with food shortages and unemployment, heavily disrupted the everyday life of millions of citizens (Jenkins 2007, 319). Between 1918 and 1919, as a third of the world's population contracted the virus, death rates grew to between five and twenty times higher than normal, with up to 100 million estimated deaths. As a result of this disastrous disruption to daily life, during the Spanish Flu there was a combination of an increased radicalization of contentious politics in various parts of the world with a fear of broad social conflicts pushing for the development of a public health system. The political attribution of the causes of the suffering triggered intense reactions, up to and including revo-lutionary events. Indeed, combined with the pressure of an expanding reform movement that had also focussed on health issues, the responses to the Spanish Flu included the establishment of public health services as well as the administration of public health by centralized governments, such that one historian has characterized it as 'an epidemic that legitimized reform' (Jenkins 2007, 337–8).

As will be argued in the following sections, the variable mix of challenges and opportunities related to a critical juncture, in this case a health emergency, had an impact on the repertoire of action, the organizational networks and the collective framing of progressive social movements that adapted to the pan-demic conditions and the related crises, but also tried to transform them.

2 Repertoires of Contention in the Pandemic: Between Disrupting and Caring

Repertoires of Contention in Times of Emergency: An Introduction

The Covid-19 pandemic has undoubtedly been a contentious period. While lockdown initially seemed to have frozen all opportunities for protest, by confining people to their homes or at least heavily constraining their ability to move freely and assemble in groups, social movements proved capable of adapting to these external circumstances that were themselves rapidly changing. As we will see in this section, a number of innovations in the repertoires of contention have built upon existing trends, consolidating rather than replacing some of these. What is more, it will be shown that collective action did not solely make use of existing resources, rather, it was successful in generating new networks and ideas.

It is not only the number of protests that can happen that is affected by intense periods, but also the forms that these protests can take. While repertoires of contention change slowly, as they are consolidated over time (Tilly 1978), cycles of protests are also sites for innovation in forms of action (Tarrow 2011; della Porta 1995; della Porta and Diani 2020, chap. 6). Indeed, repertoires of contention vary from one social movement to another and from one social movement organization to another. They are adapted to take account of the amount and type of resources available to a particular group, but also constrained by specific normative choices. In order to have an impact on their own constituencies as well as on public opinion, potential allies and governments, repertoires of action are designed according to different logics of influence. These can be summarized as: (1) a logic of number, aimed at proving how widespread certain concerns are; (2) a logic of damage, which threatens or implements behaviour that inflicts a cost on their targets; and (3) a logic of testimony, in which activists demonstrate the strength of their commitment through their levels of sacrifice (della Porta and Diani 2020). It should be noted, however, that repertoires of action are not restricted to the act of protesting in the streets, as knowledge production and solidarity activities are also very relevant factors in this process.

This section will focus specifically on repertoires of contention during the pandemic. Having put forward some expectations about the effects of the pandemic on repertoires of contention, I will present evidence on how disruptive forms of protest adapted to the threats posed by the period. These include the building of alternative knowledge by progressive social movement organizations, as well as the emergence and spread of forms of self-help.

In terms of the expectations relating to repertoires of contention in the current context, many of these derive from a consideration of the pandemic period as a period of emergency, in which progressive social movements aim to broaden their constituency by addressing various deeply aggrieved groups that they hope in turn to mobilize. Before examining the mechanics of this process, it must be noted that social movements have often been analyzed as a product of an opening up of opportunities and the availability of resources for collective action. Under conditions of expanding opportunities in particular, repertoires of contention have traditionally been oriented towards moderate forms of disruption, aimed especially at building upon an already broad constituency as well as institutional allies. Movements of 'crisis', which arise when everyday life is negatively affected in a sudden and profound manner, have instead been characterized as mainly reactive in nature. Participants in these movements, at least in the early stages, are mainly those directly affected by said change, and react with forms of protest that tend to be more spontaneous and more inclined to involve violent outbursts (Kerbo 1982, 654; della Porta 2013). In a similar vein, moments of deep economic deprivation have been considered as triggering the 'defensive behaviour of a society faced with change' (Polanyi 1957, 130).

To a certain extent, the protests that have taken place during the pandemic do seem to have been driven by a reaction to the dramatically worsening quality of life, especially in the less protected sectors of the population. Employing a mix of both new and traditional repertoires of contention, protests have even included pre-modern forms of resistance, from individual withdrawals from work to unstructured (albeit barely spontaneous) forms, such as walk-outs or sit-ins. While they have remained non-violent in nature, protests have included wildcat strikes and flashmobs, aimed at attracting attention not as a result of the number of participants but through symbolic disruption. However, this is far from the full story, and protests have emerged in multifarious and innovative forms, just as had been the case during the financial crisis. Research on the anti-austerity protests of the 2010s challenged the view of movements of crisis as weak, reactive and potentially violent (e.g. Kerbo 1982). It has been shown how, given certain political and social conditions, progressive actors have been able to develop massive and mainly peaceful protests, building upon an existing repertoire of contention that involved moments of high mobilization in rallies and strikes but also innovative forms of action, such as the protest camps, oriented to the prefiguring of alternative practices (della Porta 2015).

As had happened during the global justice movements, protest during the Great Recession was not only oriented towards putting pressure on authority by creating disruption in the public order, but also towards building public spaces for the development of alternative knowledge (della Porta 2009; della Porta and Pavan 2017). Movements that have been active on health rights, as well as on environmental or gender issues, have paid particular attention to the social construction of expertise (Snow and Lessor 2010; Taylor and Leitz 2010). The development of knowledge from below has also been particularly relevant during the pandemic, when the reliance on the digital space has expanded. Just as in the case of the anti-austerity protests, the perception of an emergency triggers the need for cognitive innovation, challenging existing paradigms and routines.

In a less visible, but equally intensive manner, social movement organizations have also been involved in forms of mutual help, which have allowed for the direct expression of solidarity through the bridging of self-help and advocacy. During the Great Recession in particular, forms of direct social action spread as ways of not only helping others, but also of reconstituting social ties and developing alternatives in action (Bosi and Zamponi 2019). Groups active on migrant conditions, gender discrimination, self-managed clinics, alternative forms of production and consumption have aimed at re-appropriating rights in what scholars like Engin Isin and Greg Nielsen (2008) have defined as *acts of citizenship*. As social science research on 'poor peoples' movements has suggested, the need to address fundamental daily emergencies pushed social movement organizations active in mobilizing the unemployed or refugees to bridge advocacy with the provision of goods and services (della Porta and Steinhilper 2021). In a similar vein to the financial crisis, these practices have also been mushrooming during the pandemic, driven by the need to respond to the immediate and urgent necessity of larger and larger groups of the population, but also to experiment with different forms of contention. During the current pandemic, there has undoubtedly been a great increase in acts of solidarity aimed at responding to the increasing needs of citizens, as well as to support groups that are often stigmatized and marginalized.

As we will see, during the pandemic the repertoires of contention have built upon previous experiences in forms that are influenced by specific challenges, such as a physical reduction of open spaces, limitations on freedoms, and the growing urgency to provide for the material needs of an increasing number of people.

In the second part of this section we will see that given the constraints on freedom of assembly and on demonstrations, disruptive forms of protest had to adapt to the rhythms and characteristics of the lockdown. During the initial phase of the pandemic in particular, this led to the spread of online forms of protest, including innovative approaches such as geolocalization around symbolic places. However, there was also a transformation of private spaces, such as balconies or windows, into public spaces through the display of banners or pictures, as well as the performance of music, theatre, sport and dancing. As soon as the lockdown restrictions were relaxed, there was a re-occupation of streets and squares, initially with symbolic acts, such as flashmobs, and subsequently through socially distanced sit-ins or marches. Throughout the pandemic, strikes were taking place not only in the workplace, but also in the form of rent strikes. In all of these circumstances, physical action was blended with virtual action, as digital technologies were used in various ways to spread images of protests.

The third part of the section will explore how, alongside protesting in the street, activists also engaged in knowledge building. They not only employed, but also updated existing platforms and devices to spread counter-information on anti-contagion measures as well as on government policies, including acts of repression. Moreover, whistleblowing was used to denounce illegitimate acts of exploitation by firms and political corruption. New technologies also helped to connect activists from different movements and in different parts of the world in the production of alternative knowledge on the causes and the consequences of the pandemic. Driven by the need to deal with an unknown situation that was causing extraordinary disruption, the bridging of expert and lay knowledge helped in the development of new ideas.

Last but not least, the fourth part of this section will focus on 'mutual aid'. It will be seen how, due to increasing inequalities and the growing demand from people in need, there was a rise in mutual aid activities, which were based on existing experiences of solidarity initiatives that were adapted to the constraints of the pandemic. The provision of food and shelter, social support and legal advice went beyond simple charity in a process of politicization of claims but also a prefiguration of alternative ways to care for others. As Martinez (2020) noted in his research on the Spanish case, '[a]n enhanced meaning of the term solidarity has thus entered the mainstream public discourse: 'mutual aid'. In addition, 'support and care networks organized by many grassroots organizations and neighbours who were not involved in politics before, added practices of reconstructing urban communities in a very different way from charities and NGOs, although many of these have also been involved (sometimes also in alliance with local governments) (Martinez 2020).

Adapting Protest during a Pandemic

The pandemic called for certain disruptive forms of contention to be adapted without, however, abandoning protest as a form of contention. On the contrary, not only was there a very intense wave of strikes from the beginning of the pandemic, but rallies, flashmobs and sit-ins also multiplied. In many countries, the pandemic triggered a cycle of protests and collective action spread quickly among different sectors of the population. As had been the case in previous emergencies, the pandemic was a critical juncture, reactivating existing forms of action, but also leading to innovative performances that were aimed at adapting to changing opportunities and constraints as well as the need to address to a potentially broad and varied constituency of groups aggrieved by the pandemic.

Street protests were modulated by the rhythm of the pandemic, blending online and offline forms of collective action. At the very beginning of the crisis, the digital space was mainly used as a substitute for the squares. Given the severe constraints and rigid protocols regarding public gatherings, several protest marches were organized as virtual events instead, exploiting the potential of new technology. One of these was the demonstration organized by the so-called White Sheets under the slogan 'health is not a commodity', which took place in several countries on 7 April 2020, World Health Day, with citizens and activists posting photos of banners and messages online. Perhaps the most notable example of a digital strike, however, was the fifth global strike against climate change, carried out on 24 April 2020 by Fridays for Future, with activists geolocalizing themselves in front of highly symbolic sites (such as the Italian parliament) as well as leaving posters in squares to highlight calls for change in environmental policies. Another example of action often organized online was rent strikes, which developed as a way to denounce the serious housing problems in many countries (Martinez 2020). The rent strike spread, initially in the United States and subsequently internationally, through the diffusion of top trending hashtags such as #RentStrike, #CancelRent, #CancelMortgages and #NoIncomeNoRent, and websites such as Rentstrike2020 and WeStrikeTogether (Massarenti 2020).

In the very initial phases of the lockdown, protests adapted to the anti-contagion restrictions with performances staged on balconies or from windows. In Belgium, for example, during the daily 8 p.m. celebration of healthcare workers, movement organizations mobilizing on health rights urged citizens to display banners outside their homes with calls 'to give more money to public hospitals'. Similarly, in Spain and Italy, activists called on citizens to use private spaces in order to promote the right to public health.

As soon as the lockdown measures were softened and as the opportunities for organizing 'socially distanced rallies' opened up, offline public rallies multiplied, taking the form of flashmobs or socially distanced marches. A particularly innovative phenomenon has been the protests against police violence and racism, such as the global mobilization around the Black Lives Matter campaign.

In Italy, for instance, the dominant form of protest in this regard consisted in protesters coming together in a public square, usually the central square in front of the town hall, the prefecture building or, where present, the American consulate or embassy. The organizers were careful to comply with Covid-19 restrictions, insisting on the wearing of face masks and on social distancing. In order to ensure the latter, in many cases organizers marked a space for each demonstrator with an 'X' on the pavement. The event usually included an eight minute and forty-five second silence, to mark the time span of George Floyd's agony. Another feature that, in retrospect, was seen by many organizers as the most important element of the protest, consisted in an open microphone, which provided a voice to those who are usually not heard. The open microphone was regularly used by migrants and/or second generation immigrants and 'black Italians' to decry their own experiences involving racist attitudes in Italy, and the impact of Italian laws that institutionalize racism (della Porta, Lavizzari and Reiter 2022).

As 2020 progressed, many observers noted an intensification of strikes, which often started in quite spontaneous ways and became more structured over time. Although they are a common form of protests in the realm of production, where they originated, strikes have also spread outside of this context. In pre-pandemic times, the strike had undergone several reincarnations in the form of social strikes called by precarious workers, but also strikes for women's rights on International Women's Day or global strikes on climate organized by Fridays for Future. Due to the immediate increase of conflicts within factories during the pandemic, strikes frequently proved to be a means to demand protective equipment, better working hours and higher salaries, or at the very least to resist attempts at increasing working hours and reducing pay. As strikes took place in the workplaces, most of which remained open, they could be, and indeed were, also organized during the lockdown. With the media focussing attention almost exclusively on the pandemic, strikes acquired visibility and often became politicized, putting pressure on governments to grant the demands of workers. Among the labour protests that took place during the very first period of the lockdown, Martinez (2020) listed the following:

- Workers' strike in the Nissan factory because the company is using the crisis as an opportunity to fire workers.
- Workers' strike in the Airbus factory due to the controversial decision made by the government regarding the license for non-essential productive activities to reopen operations.
- A similar motivation behind another strike at the Aernnova factory.

- Workers forced the Mercedes company to halt production due to the lack of safety measures during the pandemic.
- Threat of workers' strike in Glovo, Deliveroo, and UberEats due to the worsening conditions and payments during the pandemic.
- Also, as a reaction to highly precarious labour conditions, waged and self-employed workers in the culture and arts sector called to various strikes because of the lack of support from the government, and the cancellation of events sine die.

In many cases, strikes developed in tandem with other forms of resistance, adapting to the fear of contagion as well as to the difficulties that the lockdown created through the closure of schools and other public care facilities. In Belgian supermarket chains, where there is low unionization, the protest started with a high rate of absence from work, which forced employers to offer compensation bonuses in order to incentivize workers to show up at their workplaces (Workers Inquiry Network 2020, 7–8). Even where unions were present, labour contention included bottom-up forms, such as wildcat strikes and sit-downs aimed at stopping production, up to and including the threat of general strikes. According to one report, at the beginning of April 2021, at least eighty-one wildcat strikes had already been counted in the United States: '[f]rom construction workers to nurses, warehouse, transport, meatpacking, call center, carpenters, fast food, trash collectors, prisoners, and a wide range of other kinds of workers, class struggle is suddenly back on the agenda in the United States, and much of the world for that matter' (Workers Inquiry Network 2020, 53). In Italy, as elsewhere in Europe, strikes also involved vastly different categories of workers 'from taxi drivers, artisans, to dealers and street vendors and restaurateurs' (Tassinari, Chesta and Cini 2020). A symbolic general strike was launched by the rank-and-file union USB Cobas, which includes health workers, care workers, fire fighters and workers in sectors of environmental hygiene, gas and energy distribution.

Another particularly visible protest campaign, bridging on- and offline forms, was that undertaken by delivery riders, who were often not provided with protective equipment or protocols against contamination by the delivery platforms for whom they worked. As early as mid-March 2020 in Italy, delivery riders organized in grassroots organizations (i.e. Deliverance Milano, Riders Union Bologna, Riders Union Roma, Riders per Napoli–Pirate Union, and the network Deliverance Project) developed a campaign that spread video and photo testimonies in which the speakers held up signs with hashtags such as #PeopleBeforeProfit, #NotForUsButForAll, #StopDelivering (Tassinari, Chesta and Cini 2020). Strikes also took place in the agricultural sector where, given the composition of the labour force, it was specifically migrants (often undocumented and mostly in precarious working conditions) who were mobilized, bridging claims related to working conditions and broader calls for recognition. A prime example of this was the 'Strike of the Invisibles', which took place in Italy on 21 May 2020, just after the first reopening post-lockdown (Tassinari, Chesta and Cini 2020).

Thus, the disruption connected to the spread of the virus challenged the global chains of production of workers in the logistic sector, also contributing to the cross-national spread of their individual struggles. Indeed, activists claimed that

> [r]eproductive workers are now exploiting the vulnerabilities in the long and thin 'just in time' global supply chain. . . . It is this strategy of disruption at key global choke points that offers the greatest potential for turning our planet back away from its path towards ecological catastrophe. . . . As capital relies ever more on managing a global 'just in time' supply chain through the use of algorithmic data management, these relative small wildcat strikes have tipped these global corporate giants off balance. (Workers Inquiry Network 2020, 58)

The Building of Alternative Knowledge

Aside from engaging in disruptive forms of protest, social movement activists also produce alternative knowledge. While knowledge construction is central to social movements in general (della Porta and Pavan 2019) as they develop alternative codes, during the pandemic this task has become both more essential and more challenging. As in other movements around health issues, cognitive activities, in which expert and lay knowledge is combined, emerge as all the more relevant in moments of crisis. This is due to the increasing perception that the existing paradigms are no longer sufficient to understand a rapidly changing situation or act as a guide to action. This is true not only for the dominant paradigms within society, but also for those once widespread in social movements. During the Covid-19 pandemic, social movement organizations have in fact invested a lot of energy into the construction and spread of alternative knowledge, which includes counter-information and whistle-blowing activities as well as collaborative thinking aimed at the construction of alternative narratives.

With regard to *counter-information*, as media consumption temporarily intensified, digital technology helped to spread practical knowledge about how to organize everyday life during the pandemic (Trenz et al. 2020). This was especially true during the lockdown phase, in which very localized relationships, such as those between neighbours or with local shop keepers, became mediated through the use of (mainly) pre-existing apps in order to reinvent public spaces online. Acts of political consumerism spread via Instagram stickers such as 'Support Small Businesses'. In the United States, the website Support Local or Else (SLoE) repositioned local business in a new digital space with the call to action 'Do your Part. Support local.' Platforms that were already oriented towards increasing socialization among neighbours before the pandemic (such as the German Nebenan.de) in some cases politicized their activities by promoting collective action around shared concerns (Trenz et al. 2020).

A further way in which counter-information proved important was in reaching out to groups at high risk and in helping them to deal with the health crisis. In Italy, networks that provide support to migrants collected and spread information. This was done, for instance, through the publication of an open letter entitled 'CoVID-19: No one is safe until ALL are protected!', which aimed 'to raise awareness on the worsening conditions of people in transit along the route', calling for the end to dehumanizing practices targeted towards migrants (Milan 2020). In Germany, a small group of friends from various medical and social professions founded the Poliklinik, a 'solidary medical centre', whose main claim was that 'you can only change health via social conditions – we think that social determinants make you sick, like housing conditions, working conditions, racism'. Building a Covid-19 task force, they used a phone line to organize the production and distribution of face masks and information material translated into various languages about the pandemic and the government measures (Fiedlschuster and Reichle 2020). Civil society organizations were also active in the Global South, particularly in contributing to public education about security measures aimed at curbing the pandemic. Initial accounts mention that

> LIAE's public sensitization and citizen engagement for proper handwashing in Ethiopia, CSRC's food provision in Nepal, PWAN's quick response to provide communities with accurate information on COVID-19, and NETRIGHT members' fundraising and resource mobilization for women and vulnerable groups, all contribute to immediate, far-reaching, and life-saving impacts during the COVID-19 pandemic. (Landry et al. 2020)

Meanwhile, in Latin America, counter-information was important, among others, in the case of domestic care workers, to whom trade unions and volunteers addressed guidelines, 'offering advice on how to protect themselves and suggesting ways of negotiating the best possible working conditions with their employers' (Acciari 2020).

The collection of counter-information has been especially significant in the cases in which the pandemic and the lockdown measures fuelled repression oriented towards marginalized sectors of the population. One example of this is the Delhi Relief Collective in India, which had formed as a loose association of NGOs and individual volunteers to address previous crises. During the pandemic they made use of various social media platforms to collect and spread information about relief work, building databases of target beneficiaries, but also to list the changing governmental rules about the lockdown and provide information on the rampant food crisis. Working with a low-income constituency, the group built 'a rights-based discourse around the fallouts of the lockdown for informal and migrant worker', focused 'media and political attention on the situation', and advocated for 'targeted governance and emergency welfare measures' (Mohanty 2020). Similarly, along the Balkan routes taken by many refugees, a network called Border Violence Monitoring reported on episodes of police violence committed against migrants at border crossings. As a result, '[w]ith the borders closed and people locked inside their houses, those experiencing violence at the border and discriminatory treatment, mostly committed by the Croatian police, are given the possibility to send their testimonies in a safe manner by means of social networks' (Milan 2020).

Another form of knowledge spread that thrived during the pandemic is *whistleblowing*. Citizens' watch initiatives were set up to monitor both pharmaceutical corporations and state repression (Pleyers 2020), but also to inform the public about workers who had not been provided with personal protective equipment (Cox 2020). Acts of whistleblowing were performed by Egypt's healthcare workers, as nurses denounced the lack of tests and PPE with the support of the Egyptian Medical Syndicates. In this case, '[d]espite the considerable risks associated with collective direct action in an authoritarian context, digital acts of whistleblowing have coalesced into traditional forms of dissent involving collective claim making on the ground' (Sharkawi and Ali 2020). To cite another example, the Spanish Commissiones Obreras set up a free phone hotline and email account to offer workers, especially those in non-unionized companies, the possibility to report on the lack of implementation of safety protocols.

In addition to counter-information and whistleblowing, the *construction of alternative knowledge* has also been central to the development of a broader narrative of the pandemic crisis. In particular, the environmental movement, which had already begun to mobilize on climate justice, presented climate change and the pandemic as interlinking challenges. As schools and universities became less accessible, or indeed wholly inaccessible, Fridays for Future mainly moved online. Activists organized digital assemblies where they discussed perspectives and developed new proposals, such as the 'Back to the Future' programme, which focusses on a socially equitable and environmentally just response to the pandemic. Turning to social media, they invested energy into the construction of an alternative narrative, which drew on data that confirmed the connection between the environmental crisis and the health crisis, given that increasing pollution and global warming have proved conducive to the spread of the contagion. Consequently, the FFF activists promoted the hashtag #fighteverycrisis, arguing that 'instead of trying to figure out which crisis is worse, we should recognize the severity of each crisis and act accordingly to prevent them in the future'. In this direction, processes of collaborative thinking and writing led to the drafting of an open letter titled 'Degrowth: New Roots for the Economy. Reimagining the Future After the Corona Crisis', signed by more than 1,100 individuals and 70 organizations from 60 countries, which suggested five principles to guide responses to the Covid-19 crisis as well as plans for economic recovery:

> (1) Put life at the center of our economic systems, not economic growth; (2) Radically re-evaluate how much and what work is necessary for a good life for all, emphasizing care work; (3) Organize society around the provision of essential goods and services, minimizing wasteful practices; (4) Democratize societies, struggling against authoritarian and technocratic tendencies; and (5) Base political and economic systems on the principle of solidarity, rather than competition and greed. (Paulson 2020)

An equally important phenomenon has been the construction of spaces for the development of alternative knowledge for women's movement organizations, which have particularly stressed the centrality of education in promoting knowledge from below. In Mexico, for instance, where women's groups were already highly mobilized, the pandemic has provided the trigger for further knowledge building as

> online workshops, reading groups, and seminars are hosted weekly by different organizations to continue the ongoing discussions around violence, sexual harassment, job conditions, gender stereotypes, reproductive rights, and many other issues that affect women in their everyday lives. Feminist collectives, such as the hacktivist group Luchadoras, coordinate discussions and debates on how the measures implemented to control the pandemic simultaneously reflect and aggravate socio-economic, political, geographic and gender inequalities. (Ventura Alfaro 2020)

The spread of tools for encounters online has helped international connections. Transnational networks of activists have become involved in virtual conversations oriented towards the construction of alternative knowledge and innovative ideas. This was the manner in which a call for 'careful radical transformation', bridging environmental and gender concerns, was produced in March and April 2020. Around forty activists from many countries around the world took part in a series of virtual conversations 'that mixed strategizing for political change with mutual encouragement for facing immediate challenges'. After circulating ideas and drafts, the group produced two public documents – 'Feminist Degrowth: Reflections on COVID-19 and the Politics of Social Reproduction' and 'Collaborative Feminist Degrowth: Pandemic as an Opening for a Care-Full Radical Transformation' – which have been translated into several languages (Paulson 2020).

In summary, the pandemic challenged progressive social movements to undertake a great deal of investment in knowledge building, oriented towards spreading a different vision of the emerging problems and their possible solutions.

New Mutualism in the Pandemic Period

Beyond protesting in the street and building alternative knowledge, social movements also engaged in what have been considered as new forms of *mutual help*. In addition to calling for the state to intervene in crisis situations, progressive social movements have developed their own practices oriented towards directly addressing social problems by providing immediate solutions. While the development of cooperatives has been a typical activity of labour movements, women's movements and environmental movements have also experimented with alternative forms of providing assistance to their constituencies. Shortly before the pandemic, several progressive social movements – which included poor people's movements (Piven and Cloward 1977) or social movements mobilized on the social effect of the Great Recession or in support of refugees' and migrants' rights – had in fact been engaged in solidarity actions oriented to responding to the material needs of their constituencies (della Porta 2015). Self-help has also been a central factor for social movement organizations working on health issues, allowing for the transformation of stigmatized identities into positive ones (Taylor and Leitz 2010).

From the very beginning of the Covid-19 pandemic, mutual aid activities have been extremely important. While solidarity often involved homogeneous groups (such as artists, or transgender individuals), it also spread across different sectors of society. For instance, in Spain, racialized street vendors and women (such as the Sindicatos de Manteros and the Xarxa de Dones Cosidores) have manufactured face masks and other equipment to be donated to health workers (Martinez 2020), while hackers from autonomous and squatted social centres have been involved in producing medical equipment. In the Global South, where activists were often caught between the denialist politics of governments (as in Brazil, Mexico or Nicaragua) and the imposition of harsh states of exception (as in el Salvador, Honduras and Guatemala), mutual help activities quickly sprang up, such as in Brazil (FASE 2020), The Philippines (Gutierrez 2020) or India (Banarjee 2020).

In many cases, solidarity grew within local communities, at times driven by compassion, but in some cases also evolving into a political practice, which has been defined as 'a relation of a shared struggle against oppression' (Fiedlschuster and Rosa Reichle 2020). This shared struggle could be seen in several cities in Germany, for example, where activists set up 'giving fences', hanging donations at specific locations for homeless people and other people in need. Solidarity also spread at a community level in the United Kingdom, where the Covid-19 crisis provided the 'hotbed from where the mutual aid social movement was reborn'. Given 'the need for local community support groups at the micro level, to perform basic tasks for people', mutual aid groups became 'vital in collecting people's medical prescriptions, their shopping and keeping claimant's welfare benefit entitlements in payment'. Thus, the pandemic saw 'an escalation in telephone befriending by mutual aid volunteer groups, required as more people became socially isolated' (Duke 2020). This was also the case in Italy, where preexisting and newly established groups, including solidarity brigades formed by squatters and neighbourhood activists, organized home delivery and the distribution of groceries, legal support and help with accessing public services for precarious, migrant and informal workers as well as the unemployed (Non una di meno Roma).

Another context in which mutualism proved key was in the women's movement. Building upon previous practices, the activists embedded new forms of mutual aid into their longstanding and in-depth experience with self-help, in particular in relation to violence against women and sex-workers. Thus, in response to increasing economic insecurity, feminist collectives organized soup kitchens and the supply of food and essential products for those who were most affected by the crisis. Through social media, they promoted the donation of food and medicine for vulnerable citizens in precarious working conditions. Often, 'the activists are ... community members who offer their own private house to operate and distribute these goods' as well as promoting 'feminist trading through exchange of services and products' (Ventura Alfaro 2020). Beyond the provision of much needed help, these experiences became ways to prefigure alternative forms of caring. As the feminist collective Non Una di Meno Roma (2020) noted:

> Containing the contagion is not enough, we need struggles for reconfiguring the infrastructures of care, taking control away from market forces. . . . The

mutual-aid networks operating in many Italian cities point in that direction: they have developed modes of caring from below that draw attention beyond individuals and towards communities.

The reflection on caring was similarly important for the environmental movement. For instance, a call for 'Care-full radical transformation' defined the pandemic as 'a crisis of reproduction of life' which poses the need to reflect on 'the work of care: for each other as well as for the non-human world' (Paulson 2020).

There was also a concerted effort by groups active in solidarity with refugees to extend efforts to provide material help during the pandemic. An example of this is the No Name Kitchen, in which international volunteers distributed hot meals and first-aid support to undocumented migrants travelling through the Western Balkans migration route. In Trieste, the final stop on the Balkan route in Italy, the Linea d'Ombra association offered medical help to migrants reaching the city, often barefoot, after encountering police brutality on their long journey. As the founder of the association explained, '[W]e kept healing their wounds even when local authorities revoked the authorization to provide assistance to migrants on the open space, and we were asked to hide in a less visible spot' (Milan 2020). Solidarity initiatives have been particularly relevant in the Global South, focussing upon the 'immediate needs that an emergency response requires' (Landry et al. 2020). In South Africa, for instance, broad coalitions of over 300 social movement organizations converged in a network engaged in the education of disadvantaged sections of society (Alexander 2020).

As had also happened during the financial crisis, direct social action addressed the need for sociability that neoliberal capitalism had undermined (Bosi and Zamponi 2019). This was the case, for instance, in queer spaces, conceived as safe spaces, free from homo- and transphobic violence. In Berlin, a number of queer and LGBT initiatives involving hundreds of volunteers organized an ad-hoc relief line for marginalized people in the city with the objective 'to run errands and shopping trips, pre-cook and deliver meals, offer financial support, and match people with others to talk with' (Trott 2020). Platforms were also used to broadcast cultural events online and thus support artists who had become unemployed because of the pandemic.

The networking taking place among activist groups is facilitated by the full embrace of new technologies. As a volunteer of the Solidarity Kitchen in the United Kingdom explains,

> Crucial for the smooth functioning of our political infrastructures is technology. We have an open online forum where whoever is interested in joining the solidarity kitchen, or just curious about it, is able to see at a glimpse the form of our political structure, join a working group and read

the minutes of the meetings. We also make use of social media, which is key for reaching new users and recruiting participants. And of course, instant messaging apps provide a much needed bridge between political and physical infrastructures. We are aware of different degrees of confidence when using technology, so we offer personalized training to everyone interested and make sure that important information is available in different formats. A financial update is published weekly, and there is a section on the forum where all decisions are compiled, including how and by whom they were taken in order to ensure accountability. Transparency is one of our core values, and we take it very seriously. (Ruiz Cayuela 2020)

More generally, it can be said that through their actions progressive social movements have challenged the narrative of an individualized response to the crisis, such as staying at home and taking care of oneself, as '[t]he quarantine condition poses unprecedented challenges to bring out a sense of publicness – both in terms of people's concern for political and social issues and in terms of bringing issues from the private sphere to the public sphere' (Bao 2020, 60). As activists of the Solidarity Kitchen initiatives noted, their aim was to 'sketch out the world to come, carrying practices of self-organization that can potentially break with state-centred logics', against a 'political sequence that wanted to condemn us to "stay at home"' (Workers Inquiry Network 2020, 31). Solidarity initiatives so often contributed to creating trust and politicizing their message (Gerbaudo 2020; Wood 2020a and 2020b), fuelling an alternative sense of community (Pleyers 2020).

Empowering Contentious Participation in the Pandemic: Concluding Remarks

In summary, contentious politics during the pandemic took various forms. As with contentious politics in a non-pandemic period, disruptive street politics mixed a logic of numbers, to show the spread of support for their proposals (i.e. digital strikes or petitions), a logic of damage, by creating costs for their targets (i.e. workers' strikes but also the citizens' rent strikes), as well as a logic of testimony, by proving the extent of their commitment through sacrifice with the willingness to run high risks and costs for collective action (i.e. the vigil held by nurses standing in front of abusive right-wing militants) (della Porta and Diani 2020, chap. 5). However, the repertoire of protest also innovated on previous practices by adapting to constraints on the rights of movement and assembly, through blended, distanced and symbolic forms of action. In addition to this, movements also sought to broaden their potential constituency, with the aim of increasing the political participation of those sections of society that had been hit hardest by the health crisis.

However, the activities of progressive social movements during the pandemic are not limited to visible protests. By exploiting digital resources and platforms for information production and sharing, social movements have also contributed to connecting the different fields of knowledge that tend to be fragmented by the hyper-specialization of science. By intertwining theoretical knowledge with practical knowledge and experimenting with different ideas, they also aimed at prefiguring a different future.

Aside from protesting and producing alternative knowledge, progressive movements also contributed to one of the most urgent tasks in this dramatic context: the production and distribution of goods and services of different types. Faced with the limited capacity of public institutions (weakened by long-standing neoliberal policies) to respond to the crisis, activists built upon experiences of mutual help (that had already been nurtured to address the social crisis triggered by the financial crisis and especially the austerity responses to it at the beginning of the 2010s) to intervene in bringing support to those in need. As such, progressive civil society organizations and grassroots neighbourhood groups distributed food and medicines, produced masks and medical equipment, sheltered homeless people and protected women suffering from domestic violence. The principle of food sovereignty and the solidarity economy spread through practical examples as an alternative to the disrupted global food chain.

In doing so, activists have challenged a top-down conception of charity, by instead supporting norms of solidarity that contrast with the extreme individualism of neoliberal capitalism. Through social interventions, they have reconstituted relationships that had been broken well before the pandemic, but have also politicized claims, shifting from immediate relief to proposals for radical social change.

Collective action thus proved particularly important when faced with disruptive events, stimulating relational, cognitive and affective mechanisms (della Porta 2020a). At the relational level, action itself tended to produce a sort of social capital, putting individuals and organizations in contact with each other as well as creating arenas for encounters to take place. Although the emergency restricted the amount of time available to find solutions to immediate needs, the lockdown provided opportunities to engage in collective activities. Time was, however, very unequally distributed; with the closing down of schools and public care institutions, for example, care activities had to be dealt with by families themselves. There was, therefore, at the same time, a need to offer alternative care but also an increased need to receive it. At the cognitive level, the pandemic conditions disrupted normal routines and ways of thinking, driving the development of alternative knowledge, the importance of which in such uncertain times was demonstrated. At an emotional level, the emergency triggered a fear of others, but it also generated feelings of solidarity as an alternative to succumbing to despair. Intense emotions fuelled social participation as collective action was driven by indignation and compassion, motivating people to organize themselves and create solidarity networks in order to do something to participate in the collective effort against the virus (Spear et al. 2020). The street protests, the building of alternative knowledge and the practices of solidarity that have been mapped out in this section were made possible by different forms of organization – a topic that will be further explored in the following section.

3 Organizing during a Pandemic: From the Local to the Global

Organizing during a Pandemic: An Introduction

Repertoires of action are strongly related to organizational models (della Porta 2009). As protests always imply some degree of organization, waves of contention – such as the ones that have developed during the pandemic – have implications on collective mobilization. In social movement studies, organizational choices have generally been linked to both material resources and normative preferences. Since the 1970s, research and theorization has stressed the importance of available resources in the environment, considering the presence of social movement organizations as preconditions for action. However, three caveats have been introduced into the debate that have relevant implications for the understanding of contentious politics during the Covid-19 pandemic. In this section, having outlined each of these caveats, I will first look at the emergence of new organizations; then I will address the remobilization of social movement organizations from previous waves, before finally considering the ways in which networking took place during mobilization itself, triggered by the need to pool together scarce resources but also subsequently developing as an aim in and of itself.

With regard to the caveats that must be born in mind when considering contentious politics during the pandemic, the first point to make is that not all organizations pre-exist the mobilization: rather, many of them are often *created* in the heat of waves of collective action. Undoubtedly, existing social movement organizations play an important role in triggering protests. Formal and informal networks from different movements reactivate themselves or become more visible with every new tide of contention. However, cycles of protests also produce organizations and organizational innovation (della Porta 2013; Tarrow 2022). This is particularly true in the initial phase: as collective action is forced to remain focussed on the local level, mobilizations build upon grassroots groups that, although at times short-lived, nonetheless form the basis of further organizational transformation. As mobilization intensifies, the need for coordination brings about a proliferation of new networks. In adapting to the necessities of the moment, but also reflecting upon past successes and failures, old and new social movement organizations are also influenced by new generations of activists (della Porta 2009).

The second point is that social movement organizations are *players* in complex arenas (Duyvendak and Jasper 2015). Very different organizational models persist within any social movement or contentious campaign. While this plurality often brings about tensions between the different conceptions and practices of democracy embedded within different organizational models, cooperation also triggers cross-fertilization within broad social movement families. What is more, social movement organizations interact with other actors. This occurs not only in the protest arena but also at times in the representative arena, at the electoral level and in policy implementation, as well as in the market. Consequently, social movement organizations build complex relationships with other types of collective actors as they lobby the political and economic elites, intervene in a complex media environment, and put pressure on governments and commercial firms.

The third and final point is that, within neoinstitutional approaches, social movement organizations have been considered as guided not solely by strategic considerations, but also by *normative* concerns. The selection of an organizational model does not only follow rational assessments about the allocation of tasks, but is also constrained by existing organizational repertoires (Clemens and Minkoff 2007). The latter are built upon calculations of costs and benefits, as well as on criteria of appropriateness. An aspiration to experiment with participatory models of democracy has been noted for progressive social movements that often aim at prefiguring in their organizational structure the type of relationships they would like to extend to the whole of society (della Porta 2015). While these utopian visions inevitably fall short of the activists' hopes once they are implemented, they represent an important basis for any experimentation with new organizational models.

If we focus on periods of crisis, and more specifically on periods of emergency, we can expect some specific organizational dynamics to develop. In particular, the capacity to organise collectively would be made more difficult by a major disaster, as a result of both legal constraints and competition for limited resources. During an epidemic, for example, the fear of others spreads as they become seen as potential vectors of contagion. Emergencies also make intervention more urgent, meaning that pragmatic concerns might be expected to dominate under conditions of declining resources and increased needs. However, it is important to note that urgent needs might also trigger different trends. On the one hand, resourceful groups might have an advantage, given the need for professional and well-structured responses. On the other hand, however, responses might initially develop at the local level, where more emphasis is placed on practical knowledge and emotional identification. The specific conditions of a pandemic, in which restrictions are placed on both movement and gatherings, also have the potential to fuel more proximate forms of organization, blended with an increased use of digital spaces.

As with repertoires of action, the very different ways in which the pandemic affects different groups and territories may also fragment the organizational response. At the same time, however, the need to join forces can facilitate alliances in action, which also bring about potential hybridization between different organizational models. While competition can be high in such situations, a certain level of coordination can be facilitated by maintaining a pragmatic attitude. Finally, an element that is all the more important during a pandemic is the capacity to produce resources through symbolic and emotional incentives as well as the capacity to quickly adapt to changing conditions and to multiple needs and activities. In common with health movements, we might expect aggrieved groups to build self-help initiatives and professional social movement organizations to be founded by activists endowed with particular expertise (Banaszak-Holl, Levitsky and Zald 2010).

The pandemic acts as an accelerator for organizational transformations, but also, at the same time, as a consolidator of pre-existing trends. While old organizations remobilise, bringing with them specific organizational repertoires, there have also been innovations, fuelled by the speed of the decisions that have needed to be made, the heightened emotions and the urgent need to respond to continuous emergencies. A pandemic period implies working within specific conditions of forced confinement that constitute both challenges and opportunities for organisers: the former are presented by impediments on gatherings and the negative emotions that the virus triggers; the latter arise from the pressure to do something and the collective feeling of solidarity that are often prompted by disasters (Curato 2020).

Grassroots Organizing as a Reconstitution of Spaces of Sociability

Research on emergency periods has shown that, as conditions are disrupted in everyday spaces, groups of citizens may act collectively to defend them (Curato 2020). This can also be seen to be the case following the spread of Covid-19. Just as had happened during the financial crisis from 2008 onwards (Bosi and Zamponi 2019), during lockdown, solidarity campaigns developed through a proliferation of initiatives at the community level. There was, in particular, a rise in the number of solidarity groups aimed at providing mutual aid among peers as well as an increase in care activities for those sections of the population that were considered most in need. With the introduction of constraints on free movement and gatherings, the importance of the local scale increased, bringing about the spread of grassroots groups. Many organizations emerged at the local level as, under dire circumstances, 'informal solidarity groups have sprung up to provide such things as cooked hot meals, online vouchers that migrants can use to buy food locally, first aid support and much-needed information on the virus' (May Black, Chattopadhyay and Chisholm 2020). While these initially consisted of networks of friends and/or neighbours, they also collaborated with more politicised and better structured organizations, including civil society organizations already involved in solidarity activities and more politicised social movement organizations active in specific areas.

In several areas, responses to the pandemic emergency initially came about through affected individuals acting to help neighbours who were more in need, often subsequently developing ties during their joint activities. As has been noted, solidarity emerged out of the need to keep social ties active:

> [O]rdinary people – those without activist or clearly articulated coopera-tive political backgrounds and experiences – have shown an empathic response to the suffering of others during the crisis. In such cases, people are motivated to act without having connection to a formal institutional or organizational body. In many cases, involvement begins as simply responding to expressions of need by running errands, empathic listening over the phone or via online connections, or helping to shovel a driveway.
>
> (May Black, Chattopadhyay and Chisholm 2020)

Friendship played an important role in originating several such grassroots groups. This was the case, for instance, with a Telegram chat group named Leipzig Ost Solidarisch (Leipzig East Solidarity), which was initially founded by three friends and went on to number 860 members. The group worked on the platform to share information, which 'ranged from inspirational leaflets from groups in other cities to comics for explaining COVID-19 to kids, and flyers with hotlines about domestic violence' (Fieldschuster and Reichle 2020).

In these contexts, grassroots organizing brought about the construction of much-needed organizational spaces, given the heavy constraints on the use of the most traditional places for protest activities: the streets and the squares. During the strictest months of lockdown in particular, much protest was self-organised at a very local territorial scale, demonstrating the potential for aggregation in physical spaces, even during the hardest moments of the first lockdown. In many European cities, balconies became sites of resilience and socially distanced aggregation, functioning as a social space for communica-tion, and even as 'sites of contention' (Aronis, 2009). During the period of confinement, balconies made it possible to revive relationships with others through dance, theatre or collective poetry readings (Calvo and Bejarano 2020). In Spain, Belgium and Italy, as well as in New York City, from the very first weeks of the lockdown, 'a growing number of individuals started to play their music after the minutes of collective applause to express gratitude towards health workers and doctors', with many such performances subsequently being shared on social media (Calvo and Bejarano 2020). In fact, playing music on balconies has been defined as a relational practice that fuels the creation of social capital as it

> expresses the search of communities to find collective ways of handling disaster. Performers played motivated by the idea to build a sense of collective strength. Individuals played while neighbours listened, one day after another. They kept playing because neighbours (and later on followers in social media) asked them to do so, sometimes explicitly in the form of balcony to balcony requests of specific music, sometimes by social media or other means. Very often performers and audiences were not acquainted. But they had connected visually thanks to their balconies and the musical experience (Calvo and Bejarano, 2020).

In all cases, thanks to its capacity to develop bonds between strangers, music contributed to the spread of a sense of interconnectedness, thus alleviating the solitude and sadness of the lockdown (Calvo and Bejarano 2020).

There was also an increase in grassroots organizational forms during labour mobilizations, especially in the least unionised sectors, which were often on the frontline during the pandemic. Both in the United States and elsewhere, self-organization in the work place was pivotal in fostering several wildcat strikes at the very beginning of the pandemic, such as those organised by the UNITE HERE union of workers in the recreational sector. Activists praised 'Self-Organizing': '[a]s nearly all the workers going on wildcat strikes are not formally in unions, most likely have their own unknown committees in the workplace, they are not limited by federal or state labor laws, union contracts, or other control mechanisms' (Workers Inquiry Network 2020, 56).

A prime example of this grassroots mobilization is the protest by call centre workers in Brazil. A worker at the Atento call centre (which provides services to several multinational corporations) recalls as follows a self-organised strike in March 2020, pointing to the pressure coming from below as worker's fears for their own lives triggered a local mobilization:

> [W]e are receiving desperate workers' complaints about the situation . . . The situation is dramatic. Ever since COVID-19 cases increased, call centre operators are being fired and disappearing from their workstations . . . In addition, those who stay are obliged to accept a work schedule on alternate days, without the right to a food allowance on break days. . . . Faced with this

absurd situation of inhumanity, workers demand a total and immediate interruption of activities. (Workers Inquiry Network 2020, 70–1)

Subsequently, digital media were used to call on people to gather in protest, often succeeding in mobilizing large groups of workers, as the protest itself created a sense of a shared destiny:

A WhatsApp group was created on 17th of March 'Atento pro Corona #2'. . . . The demonstration was scheduled for the 19th of March. It was due to start at 2:30pm, but I arrived early (1pm) to join the others. When I arrived the large number of people surprised me, I did not imagine that people with limited moments of pauses, which normally prevented them from even going to the bathroom, would take their 5-minute break to fight for rights. Not counting those who left their homes, even outside their office hours and took the bus, they stopped doing anything else to be participating. I realized that there were others in the same situation as mine, I could feel that the concern about the country's situation and our working conditions was widespread. The cries of the demonstration stretched across the block, people left the balconies of the buildings. It was then that we decided to block part of the traffic on the street. (Workers Inquiry Network 2020, 74)

In summary, it has been claimed by activists that '[t]housands of initiatives at food, energy, water, and other forms of community sovereignty across the world show that localised but interconnected solutions can work' (Kothari 2020). Through these activities, citizens reconstruct public spaces. As shown by a report on France at the beginning of the pandemic, '[s]olidarity ties are developing and strengthening, at the level of neighbourhoods, streets and buildings. Tasks that used to be the responsibility of a confined state management or privatised inside the nuclear family space, and whose assignment to certain social groups was normalised, are now the object of an explicitly collective organization' (Workers Inquiry Network 2020, 30). The ties among those involved were created by acting with others, and this was then spread further through social media.

Organizational Appropriation

Cycles of protest often trigger a transformation of existing social movement organizations as they interact with new groups (della Porta 2009). Contentious politics during the pandemics intensified through the remobilization of existing organizations, which, however, underwent transformation as part of their common campaigns. The emergency led grassroots groups to interact with groups that already existed, producing a number of transformations in the organizational field. As has been noted, '[t]imes of prolonged and profound crisis, like the current pandemic, engender the discovery of a variety of alternative arrangements of protest, mutual aid, solidarity, self-management, self-mobilization and self-organization. The pandemic has introduced a plethora of new technologies for online mobilizations by ordinary people, workers, unions, alliances, and NGOs' (May Black, Chattopadhyay and Chisholm 2020).

It can be seen that, in action, grassroots groups interacted with more structured groups. Dynamics of organizational appropriation, through the remobilization of old groups in new forms, emerged in campaigns on labour issues as strikes sprang up spontaneously, pushing existing unions to subsequently join them. In the United States, for instance, labour conflicts saw the interactions between rank-and-file groups and trade unions. This was also the case in Europe, where as early as the second and third week of March 2020,

> wildcat strikes broke out in many factories and logistics warehouses around the country, with workers walking out to demand the immediate implementation of health and safety measures that could guarantee safe working conditions. In some factories with high unionization and strong trade union presence, these mobilizations resulted in the temporary suspension of production, or at least prompted management to re-organise production process drastically to guarantee safe working conditions . . . . In face of emerging mobilizations from below and threats of a general strike leveraged by the rank-and-file union movement, the major unions also came round to calling for the closure of all non-essential productive activities. (Tassinari, Chesta and Cini 2020)

Examples such as the mobilizations of the United Electrical, Radio and Machine Workers of America and the Democratic Socialists of America in support of the grassroots organization of wildcat strikes show the potential for grassroots groups to engage with more established ones in campaigns on common issues. Similarly in Italy, more established organizations were pushed to mobilize after protests spread at the grassroots level in the logistics sector, where workers felt particularly at risk of infection given their unhealthy working conditions in which there were particularly high levels of infection. While protest events (e.g. at Amazon) were initially organised in decentralized and horizontal forms, they subsequently gained support from the grassroots unions first, and then by the main union confederations (Tassinari, Chesta and Cini 2020). Larger unions in particular mobilised to demand the enforcement of health-and-safety standards, but also developed forms of self-help and offered material support through the expansion of sick leave, and extended coverage for the self-employed, through the use of their own funds as well as through agreements with firms and governments.

Beyond trade unions, the pandemic saw the remobilization of social movement organizations that had addressed previous crises, such as the financial crisis and related austerity, bringing with them certain organizational practices. In Spain, social movements that had developed during the anti-austerity protests of the early 2010s on housing, gender and migrant rights 'created the social connections, the practical knowledge, and the discursive frames that made many of the present mobilization possible', with 'different grassroots platforms ... converging with one another, and sometimes also with more institutional organizations and public authorities' (Martinez 2020). In France, the Yellow Vests campaigned against what they called the 'Macron-virus', linking the mishandling of the pandemic with broader issues of social injustice and repression (Petitjean 2020). In the United States, left-wing groups have played an important role in the organization of the rent strikes, as '[d]espite often being marginal, these organizations prove strong offline ties and ideology, as well as experienced background in social activism' (Massarenti 2020).

In several countries, feminist collectives formed the basis for organizational innovations in the development of care from below. In Switzerland, mobilizations on women's issues developed around the Frauen*streik, which bridged trans-local policy conversations with global human rights (Thieme and Tibet 2020). Similarly, in Latin America, women's collectives have expanded their capacity to reach different constituencies and to connect them by creating 'solidarity networks across the country to attempt to tackle the gravest socioeconomic consequences of the virus at the local level: food, medicine, and other essential product shortages, amidst the rise in domestic and family violence' (Ventura Alfaro 2020). These new organizational experiences have contributed to experiments around caring, given the fact that 'moving beyond the enclosed space of the hospital, which, to be sure, is essential at the time of such a sanitary emergency, care has become a matter of diffuse and promiscuous relations, nurtured by networks of intimacy that do not coincide with biological kinship' (Non una di meno-Roma 2020, 114).

Innovation around caring activities was also central for some environmentalist movements, which were driven by the challenges posed by the pandemic to adapt their previous forms of action, expanding their reach and increasing their networks. In the first months of the Covid-19 crisis especially, many climate justice groups made an effort to support local communities. Some environmental groups coordinated with local food banks and supermarkets, delivering supplies to costumers in need or creating solidarity funds. A horizontal self-governance system of producers and consumers was seen as a way to 'work and walk together toward a de-centralised and real economic and ecological sustainable food system' (Diesner 2020). As the president of a network in Switzerland noted, producers from the sustainable farming organization Community Supported Agriculture (CSA) had to change their practices, from changing their delivery system to managing volunteers. It is super complicated but at the same time very exciting, because everybody seems to realise that we play a big part in providing healthy food to the city population. With the closed borders, huge vegetable growers have had employment problems as they usually hire temporary, foreign, low cost workers and we, as CSA groups, don't. (URGENCI 2020)

Protests also built upon previous waves of mobilization in the Global South, helping to foster further organizational networking. This can be seen, for example, in India, where groups mobilised to further extend emergency help that they were already active on against discrimination of migrant labourers on issues such as starvation, homelessness, commuter transportation, sexual violence, labour rights and Islamophobia. A prime example of this was the joint action committee that had formed during the anti-CAA movement and developed into a spontaneous common platform for relief during the coronavirus crisis, working around community kitchens established by Muslim youth (Mallige and Thapliyal 2020).

Networking in Action

As organizational models adapt to growing and diverse constituencies, emergency periods are a time in which alliances can develop out of the need to provide solutions for urgent problems. Indeed, during the pandemic, social movements have created and strengthened alliances, 'while building upon existing social and community networks ... making connections, reinforcing pre-existing associations and solidarities, and reproducing what has already been established as a community's strength in the face of adversity/ies' (May Black, Chattopadhyay and Chisholm 2020). Alliance-building emerged especially around the construction of campaigns on shared concerns. In particular, networks have consolidated around an idea of solidarity as self-help, which activists have explicitly distinguished from top-down charity activities. Thus, in Spain, which was hit particularly hard by the virus, from the very start of the crisis there was an increase in care networks, organised around platforms such as *Frena la Curva* (Stop the Curve), which formed links with other groups dealing with specific aspects of the emergency. Expanding needs fuelled an intensification of interactions among different movement organizations, addressing different constituencies and reflecting on practices that made it possible to help reconstitute social ties that risked being broken by the emergency. In fact,

[f]rom the first days of the lockdown, most grassroots politics focused on discussing how the most vulnerable people, those without a home, could be sheltered, how those with casual jobs would face their contracts being

terminated immediately, and how those in overcrowded prisons and migrant detention centres would cope with the new risks and rules. This was the beginning of a powerful campaign of solidarity that was increasingly widening its range in order to include concerns for the elderly, disabled, and people otherwise at risk; concerns over domestic gender violence, and the situation of workers on various fronts, as well as children. (Martinez 2020)

The concept of the right to health provided a shared master frame for those networks dealing with specific needs triggered by the pandemic. From the outbreak of the virus, interactions intensified in this fashion through intersecting links across different social movement networks. For instance, the hashtag #LeaveNoOneBehind was spread across Europe by climate justice groups who mobilised in solidarity with refugees in a campaign to close forced camps (Thompson 2020). Another example of activists responding to an increasing need for help is on the Balkan route, where the pandemic has multiplied networking among the many pre-existing groups working in solidarity with migrants, who came together to found the Transbalkan Solidarity Network (Milan 2020).

Similarly, protests on environmental issues spread through the networking of groups striving for alternative forms of production and consumption, who became increasingly relevant during the pandemic. In Italy, for instance, the local food economy grew through the increasing ties between producers and consumers (Diesner 2020). This also happened on labour issues, as in the United Kingdom, '[w]orker action groups, cooperatives and alliances which pre-COVID-19 didn't exist, have coordinated collective action digitally on social network platforms, promoting campaign messages' (Duke 2020). These efforts are oriented towards keeping solidarity ties alive as '[n]otwithstanding the social distancing experience, emotional bonds are re-created by sharing life stories, testimonies of violence, emotions, and feelings about the quarantine, building community in the shape of new collective digital memory' (Ventura Alfaro 2020).

Indeed, it would seem that organizational networking has developed out of the mushrooming of grassroots groups, fuelled by and in turn fuelling a sense of community. To give but one example, solidarity economy initiatives in Greece used social media to develop a campaign to promote a national network and to cultivate direct local links between producers and consumers. As one activist recalled, the pandemic was perceived as a chance to broaden the target market of potential consumers:

> Out of the blue, without any access to resources or prior organization, at a time of extreme uncertainty, we were able to organise four different groups, working on aspects of the campaign, including content creation, dissemination, liaising with producers and organising the final 'match-making'. The main message of the campaign is: Support local small food production.

We are staying in our fields and cater for your household needs. We aim to reach a much larger audience than the 'usual receptors' of similar actions organised by eco-activists and bio-farmers in the past. We are addressing the average coronavirus 'quarantinees': consumers living in urban setting (from big cities to small towns), who are now concerned about the safety in big crowded stores; are interested in eating healthy; and wish to protect and cater for their families in times of uncertainty. (Gkougki 2020)

Thousands of mutual aid groups in the United Kingdom either started with Facebook groups for large areas, and then broke down into increasingly smaller groups, or organised at a very localised scale through several WhatsApp groups, which sometimes converged on specific activities at a broader level. Thus as one activist recalled, '[t]he Facebook group became so large it split into groups (our group covered an area where about 30,000+ people live). Again, this group split into 18 different local groups. We are now in a WhatsApp group with 50+ members that covers the three streets around the tower block we live in' (Workers Inquiry Network 2020, 50).

Innovative organizational trends developed from the interconnection of different experiences around global campaigns. An effect of the networking of new local groupings has been the development of mutualistic activities, which combined a pragmatism that derived from the urgency to respond to the keenly felt necessity to broaden constituencies with a normative concern with horizontality. This emerged, for instance, in the account of a volunteer from the previously mentioned Solidarity Kitchen in the United Kingdom:

We work on an ideally horizontal but practically layered structure of decision-making in which decisions are made by a mix of consensus and pressing-need. The main decisions are made in open online meetings that take place usually weekly. For smaller issues related to the daily operations we have created working groups that have a certain degree of autonomy and specific tasks assigned. We also hold regular feedback meetings with participants, where important operational issues are raised but also bring humanity and care to the tasks of the people involved. The assessment of the operations in the open meetings allows all members to reflect on the general direction of the project, but also on specific practical matters. Thus, the fluid interaction between open meetings, working groups and participants avoids the accumulation of power and ensures that the political orientation of the project remains in the correct path. It is important to acknowledge that all political infrastructures are open, and we encourage both participants and users of the kitchen to join a working group and attend to the organising meetings. (Pirate Care Syllabus, n.d.)

Thus, what were initially almost spontaneous activities often subsequently grew into more conscious and political choices, with a certain amount of transformation in the conception of the organizations themselves.

Besides offering much needed help, these initiatives engaged in bottom-up processes, both experimenting with and promoting a participatory model of internal decision-making. In the words of the activists themselves,

> movements produce resilience by resisting in imaginative and inspired ways that flow from the 'bottom-up', rather than the typical imposition of 'top-down' policies familiar to state and business organizational settings. . . . Such collective solidarity movements might thus provide a necessary contrast to the measures taken by authoritarian states in their repressive response to the crisis of the pandemic. . . . The crisis has illuminated how solidary work requires creativity, cooperative input on aims and goals and participatory action, from-below. (May Black, Chattopadhyay and Chisholm 2020)

In some groups, there was an explicit theorization of grassroots organizing as a reaction to the individualistic tendencies that were being exacerbated by the pandemic. Thus, solidarity initiatives, which reacted to the confinement imposed by fear of contagion and the orders to shelter in place, were praised as attempts to maintain forms of sociality that can sustain a sense of community. For instance, in the Collective Action Nightlife Emergency Fund in Berlin, which was founded to provide support for artists and clubs, a rotating committee was established with the task of distributing the funds that had been raised. Similar organizational structures were developed to provide for the livestreaming of music events, performances and DJ sets from clubs around the city, which was seen as providing an opportunity to come together in the face of forced solitude (Trott 2020).

Concluding Remarks

In summary, the pandemic period has seen the development of many different types of activity as organization took many different forms. In the organizational development of progressive social movements during the Covid-19 pandemic, three main trends are worth noting: (1) the flourishing of new grassroots initiatives, (2) the remobilization of different types of social movement organizations from previous waves and (3) intense networking.

Firstly, the immediate response to the needs and claims induced by the pandemic was grassroots organizing. Self-help activities mobilised small groups of friends, especially at a neighbourhood level. Since the very beginning of the pandemic, social movement organizations have mobilised in their thousands to provide mutual aid (Pleyers 2020). Organised in a bottom-up fashion, they have made significant and innovative use of social media (Kavada 2020). Initially these groups were oriented towards responding to urgent needs and were driven by spontaneous feelings of solidarity, however, they often broadened their scope and became more structured. Across the world, local initiatives have been seen as practicing a counterhegemonic emotional culture against narcissism and individualism (Gravante and Poma 2020). Born out of intimate relationships and a desire to express solidarity, they tended to grow in scale, reproducing community ties that had become jeopardized by the pandemic. In this sense, organizational models adapted to contextual constraints, but also produced and reproduced social relations among participants (Blee 2012).

Secondly, from the very beginning of the crisis, grassroots groups interacted with more politically oriented social movement organizations that had already been active in various fields of contention. These social movement organizations, struggling for gender rights, environmental concerns, and on labour and social issues, brought with them not only mobilization resources, but also normative considerations. Indeed, they reflected and spread organizational models rooted in the ideas of participatory and deliberative democracy that were already at the centre of the practices and conceptualizations of progressive movements (della Porta 2015). Although aware of the difficulties with implementing these in practice, the social movement organizations brought with them the experience of both failure and success in this regard.

Thirdly, grassroots groups have also interacted with pre-existing groups, with intense networking across movements and organizations. The collaboration between social movement organizations active on food, housing, health and environmental justice has built upon existing ties, as well as upon the action of self-help among restaurant workers, street sellers or domestic workers, who networked via zoom (Krinski and Caldwell 2020) as 'new unlikely alliances' formed to implement 'people-centered' human rights from below (Smith 2020). While networking is a common organizational process for social movement organizations, such challenging times would seem to increase the effort required to build coalitions aimed at addressing powerful targets and challenging unacceptable circumstances (van Dyke and McCammon 2010). Networking, initially driven more by necessity than by choice, gradually become more and more legitimized as it helped to bridge constituencies and concerns, contributing to the strengthening of affective ties and the bridging of cognitive visions.

As part of this process, we have seen both continuities as well as the potential for innovation in organizational formats. Transformation such as the re-comunalization of social life, the relocalization of social practices, the strengthening of autonomy and de-colonialization have been mentioned as potential outcomes of these struggles (Escobar 2020), with the possibilities for social movements to exploit cultural innovations (Ibarra 2020) and a need to reset practices of organization and communication (Castells 2020).

As we will see in the next section, these organizational choices were influenced by the narratives of the pandemic that progressive movements constructed through their framing processes.

4 Claiming and Framing in the Pandemic: From Fragmentation to Convergence

Claiming and Framing in the Pandemic: An Introduction

Waves of contention both require and contribute to the spreading of specific claims as well as to the attempt at bridging frames and innovating them. Within social movement studies frames have been considered as playing a fundamental role in the move from structural grievances to collective action. In order for a grievance to emerge, a specific strain has to be cognitively linked to criticism of the manner in which authorities treat social problems on the basis of assessments of violation of widespread principles (Klandermans 2013b, 5). While grievances often originate in material conditions, building upon feelings of dissatisfaction, resentment or indignation, the decision to mobilize on them requires cognitive processes that produce an assessment of procedural injustice (Snow 2013). In general, the responsibility for the unpleasant situation is attributed to a deliberate producer (Klandermans 2013a). Even more than the assessment of one's own interest, normative concerns have to be taken into account as action comes 'in fear and moral indignation, not in calculated efforts at personal gain' (Jasper 1997, 3).

In this section, I will begin by presenting a number of reflections on the specific relevance of framing in emergency-related critical junctures. Following this, I will then look at the main demands and discourses of progressive social movements on issues of labour rights, social justice, environmental crisis and democracy, with a particular consideration of how the main problems are diagnosed and what solutions are proposed.

In times of crisis, framing is all the more relevant given the high levels of uncertainty and consequently the need to find explanations for unknown situations. Exceptional social dislocations are expected to push disadvantaged groups into action in order to defend their subsistence and everyday routines (Snow et al. 1998). As crises are endogenous constructions of exogenous shocks (Widmaier et al. 2007), they 'unleash short bouts of intense ideational contestation in which agents struggle to provide compelling and convincing diagnoses of the pathologies afflicting the old regime/policy paradigm and the reforms appropriate to the resolution of the crisis' (Hay 2008, 68).

When it comes to movements on health issues, it can be generally said that they address the fundamental challenge of reframing the meaning of an illness, moving from individual experiences with the disease to a politicization of the definition of the causes for the personal health condition (Taylor and Zald 2010). Indeed, the framing of specific health hazards determines the prospective for collective action through alignment, but also through misalignments with general norms (Snow and Lessor 2010). In this way, activists aim at transforming stigmatised identities related with some specific sicknesses (e.g. in the case of self-help experiences), but also at thematizing health inequalities, in a broader conceptualization that opposes specialization, privatization and the fragmentation of public health. Thus, '[c]ultural beliefs about diseases and the professional authorities shape the illness experience for the affected population as well as the willingness for the affected individuals to politicize their personal experience' (Levitsky and Banaszak-Holl 2010, 15). Criticizing a one-size-fits-all conception of medicine, the anti-standardization movement has, in fact, put forward demands of participation by women and ethnic minorities against individualistic approaches (Epstein 2010).

A deeply felt disruption of daily routines is all the more important for contentious politics during the pandemic, as health injustice emerges as an important master frame for mobilization, triggering moral shocks (Gamson, Fireman and Rytina 1982; Gamson 2013, 607). By dramatically disrupting the everyday life of a large part of the population, the pandemic adds value to the meaning-making work of progressive social movements. During the disruptions caused by the pandemic, 'ongoing disputes become accentuated and new ones may arise, as actors try to adapt or reinvent their existing blueprints to conditions of uncertainty' (Aber, Rossi and von Bulow 2021). The Covid-19 pandemic has undoubtedly already been the subject of fiercely fought symbolic struggles as,

> [s]haping a 'provisional consensus' on the narrative of the COVID-19 crisis is a major stake for social movements. In the coronavirus crisis too, status quo defenders have framed the 'return to normal' as the reason to unite behind their leadership and vision. State leaders call to a 'national unity' bringing together policymakers, corporations, workers and the population in times of emergency. Activists insist on the opposite, that the reality they present as 'normal' is part of the problem and is not the only possible exit. (Pleyers 2020)

As has been outlined in the previous sections, the spread of the virus has prompted various types of protests, with progressive social movements pointing to the impact of inequalities on the rate of contagion as well as on the seriousness of the illness. A narrative of health injustice has emerged especially in the mobilizations on labour rights, but also in those on social security, which are connected to rights to health as well as education, housing, transport, etc. It has been noted that 'the sanitary emergency caused by the COVID-19 pandemic has not been simply a smooth process of top-down measures for containing it', but has rather triggered a strong wave of contestation. Thus, activists have observed,

> [r]ather than a passive path towards 'national unity' to confront with the 'invisible enemy' of this new 'war' . . . , we have seen heterogeneous forms of riots in jails, mass abstention to work, strikes, solidarity actions, forms of protest, that have make visible how, even within a pandemic, inequalities and injustices still play a crucial role in forming our contemporary societies. In other words, the 'exception' represented by the eruption of COVID-19 has enlightened the 'normal' ways in which people are hierarchized. (Workers Inquiry Network 2020, 33)

During the pandemic, contentious politics involved a large amount of specific claims bridging various rights, brought about by social groups with different capacities for (and constraints upon) cross-issue bridging. New frames that are specific to the Covid-19 crisis have been built upon already widespread ones, thus constructing a narrative of social injustice that was certainly resonant with emerging knowledge about the unequal impact of the virus. In terms of the different issues on which movements had already mobilized, the mainstream argument embodied in the slogan 'we are all in this together' has been contested by exposing the unequal consequences of both the health crisis and the social and economic crises that it triggered or, better, deepened.

As will be seen in what follows, while framing is relevant for all movements at all times, a pandemic period brings with it the additional challenge of developing a narrative that is able to connect the various specific and urgent claims of an increasingly fragmented society, combining a denunciation of multiple inequalities with the building of solidarity ties. While the virus challenged existing cognitive structures, the multiplication of the sources of inequality risked jeopardizing identification processes and the struggle for survival to prompt an atomized reaction. Additionally, during emergencies it is essential to convince a shocked public of the political implications of the problem. Looking backwards, as well as forwards into an uncertain future, social movement organizations mobilizing during a pandemic must construct a vision of a shared destiny and a common goal, which not only builds upon the traditions of progressive social movements but also innovates them. Indeed, this has been done in relation to some of the main concerns for labour rights, social rights, environmental protection, repression and democracy.

Claiming Labour Rights

Framing activities in the struggles on labour rights must address this complex situation with high levels of mobilization, but also high levels of diversity as, generally speaking, the pandemic has increased worker fragmentation along different lines. There is no doubt that workers did find themselves in largely different situations – especially so during the periods of lockdown. Some could maintain their entire salary, in many cases even working remotely; those with regular contracts were put into furlough schemes, thus losing part of their salary; precarious workers were often left without any source of income and with inconsistent access to social benefits; autonomous workers often went bankrupt; workers in small companies (especially in the tourism and cultural sectors) often became unemployed.

As a result of this, claims varied greatly according to the specific conditions addressed by workers in each sector, but also found some common ground. First of all, in an environment already characterized by protests against precarity and exploitation, the pandemic has fuelled heated debates on labour and labour rights, touching on working conditions but also the broader meaning of work itself. The definition of 'essential workers', who were excluded from the lockdown, pointed to a reversal of the traditional hierarchy, with workers in more humble conditions (such as shop assistants or couriers) being seen as the most important for collective survival in the emergency situation.

In general, labour rights were immediately linked to the right to a safe working environment. The pandemic, in fact, brought about a high risk of contamination in the work place and a worsening of working conditions, as employers often tried to increase work hours, while at the same time reducing the minimum hourly guaranteed income, sometimes providing no (or only minimal) support in the case of illness caused by Covid-19. When lockdown measures came to an end, the application of health and safety regulations during the return to work also became a widespread claim. While unionized work places were often successful in negotiating firm-level agreements on the reorganization of work time and operational procedures, protests were frequently ignored or even repressed in un-organized sectors. Campaigns, therefore, also addressed the lack of respect for workers' rights, including the right to form trade unions.

An area in which action on labour rights was immediately visible was the logistics sector, where claims addressed the definition of 'essential' activities as well as the provision of protective equipment in a sector in which the pandemic brought about a sudden increase in the demand for services. This was particularly the case in relation to freight forwarders and couriers, whose working conditions are characterized by increasing automation, digitalization and related pervasive forms of surveillance. The right to health at work, therefore, became a central frame. In Italy, on 22 March 2020, a prime ministerial decree entitled 'Chiudi Italia' (Close Italy) declared that the transport and logistics sectors were essential services that must be kept open, regardless of the goods being delivered. In warehouses and within logistics firms, workers engaged in strikes and blockades calling for social-distancing measures in storage facilities, sanitization, and the distribution of plastic gloves and protective masks. All over Italy, logistics firms such as GLS, TNT, DHL, BRT and Amazon faced strikes, with workers demanding the right to health at work, including the stipulation that they only be required to deliver essential commodities (Workers Inquiry Network 2020). Similarly, struggles developed in supermarkets and grocery stores, as the retail distribution of food and essential daily products was also considered a top priority. In Belgium, for instance, collective protests involved workers in large supermarket chains characterized by very low wages and precarious forms of work contracts, who protested (at times successfully) against the lack of provision of basic protective equipment and dangerous working conditions (Workers Inquiry Network 2020).

Health rights were undoubtedly the central frame in the struggles of workers in hospitals and residencies for the elderly, where collective opposition to the privatization of the public health system was often already ongoing. In many countries, workers in the health sector payed the highest toll in terms of work-related deaths, while workloads increased dramatically, paid leave was cancelled, and volunteers (often former healthcare workers) were asked to work for free. Nurses and medical doctors, working in both the public and private sectors, complained about low pay and bad working conditions, as well as the effects of the commodification of public health more generally. An example of this can be seen in Italy, where 100,000 doctors signed a petition calling for a territorially decentralized organization of health service provision. In the United States, nurses staged peaceful stands-ins against radical right-wing activists defying public health rules.

A narrative of acquired visibility was particularly present in the workers' struggles in the health system. This was encapsulated by a banner erected outside Vercelli hospital, in the Piedmont region of Italy, which read 'Before, we were invisible. Now we are heroes. Stop the hypocrisy, we are just workers' (Tassinari, Chesta and Cini 2020). Similarly, the movement network La Santé en Lutte in Belgium challenged the rhetoric of 'heroes on the frontline', calling for investment in public health and the requisition of private clinics and equipment. Their slogan 'Our lives are worth more than their profits', according to activists, 'clearly marks the awareness of being sacrificed on the frontline of the emergency as a consequence of the inadequacy of the government in handling the situation, but also of having to pay with their physical health and their lives as a result of decades of cuts and neoliberal policies' (Workers Inquiry Network 2020, 10).

More generally, workers in different sectors reacted to what they perceived as increasing exploitation, claiming that the state of emergency was used to reduce workers' rights. In France, the Health Emergency Law was denounced as suspending existing labour legislation, and consequently increasing work hours to up to sixty hours per week in the so-called essential sectors, which included some of the most exploited salaried workers in the logistics and the agri-food industries (Workers Inquiry Network 2020). In many countries, workers whose workplaces were forced to close called for unemployment benefits and migrant workers in the agriculture sector asked for social protection.

The challenges to the rights of workers in the most precarious conditions have been stigmatized in collective actions by domestic workers, who claimed that they were more exposed to infection and increasingly exploited or made unemployed. In Brazil, 'Cleonice Gonçalves, present!' became the main mobilizing slogan on the WhatsApp groups of domestic workers, successfully bridging social injustice with health hazards. Cleonice Gonçalves, a black woman and domestic worker, was one of the first victims to die of Covid-19 in the country, after she was infected by her wealthy employer who had just returned from a journey abroad. Her death, in contrast to the survival of her employer, was held up as evidence that coronavirus was not hitting everyone equally: '[w]hile the middle and upper classes can easily protect themselves in spacious houses, with the option of home office, social isolation is much more complex for the popular classes who are forced to stay in work, and face precarious living and housing conditions' (Workers Inquiry Network 2020). The framing, therefore, stressed the intersectional inequalities that affected domestic workers, as Cleonice Gonçalves was presented as 'the typical example of this precarious working class, exposed to high risks of contamination and without adequate social protection: they are black women, poor, with an average income below the minimum wage, often heads of their households, and located in the informal sector' (Acciari 2020).

With regard to those workers who could work remotely, collective claims have denounced over-exploitation and surveillance, framed as a consequence of the mismanagement of the pandemic. In many cases, there have been complaints that working from home involves more intense working days as new remote working software (such as monday.com) have been experimented with in order to centralize workflows. In response to this, workers' collectives complained that '[m]any are being made to work harder and faster by bosses for fear that they would be slacking off at home. The threat of layoffs or furloughing means the pressure has not lessened. Facilitated by shiny new Silicon Valley tech, old forms of surveillance are being reanimated. ... The app tracks, down to the second, the time spent working, as well tracking other key performance indicators' (Workers Inquiry Network 2020, 49). A similar claim was also made by workers at universities, where in many cases the crisis was exploited to stop collective action and to force teaching staff to work overtime as classes moved online. Activists have denounced what they see as 'yet another form of exploitation, as well as a profound discrimination against those who carry the burden of caring for children, the elderly, the disabled' (Non Una Di Meno Roma 2020), which has been promoted under the glamorous term of 'smart working'.

While specific claims were mobilized by different constituencies, the pandemic also created some occasions for alliances through frame bridging:

> The COVID-19 crisis helped increase recognition that support workers and cleaners, are as equally valuable in our society as other workers. There have been changing solidarities as new stakeholders have developed. Unusual alliances have formed e.g. food suppliers for conferences and one off events, found themselves in the same boat as make-up artists and hairdressers. Piece workers in the textile industry or wedding sector were similarly aligned, being self-employed individuals working in the gig economy. COVID-19 reignited the formation of multidisciplinary worker alliances and cooperatives ... Self-employed people in media and marketing sector, formed action groups with piece workers from the carpentry and metalworker sectors. (Duke 2020)

While the protesters commonly employed a language of violated rights in their framing, a few explicitly embraced an anti-capitalist narrative, developing 'as a direct opposition to the key operations of the neoliberal alliance between global corporations and political elites' (Martinez 2020). Demands have been put forward that address the very meaning of labour, as can be seen in calls for 'the immediate reconversion of production chains, for example of cars, towards goals that require common life to be based on reproduction and not on monetary valorization: "Let us produce respirators, not cars!"' (Workers Inquiry Network 2020, 18).

In summary, as the spread of the virus increased the suffering of workers that were already extremely exploited, what were once 'invisible' professions acquired central social value and visibility. This has been the case of workers in healthcare, logistics, retail distribution, agricultural and food industries, and waste disposal, which are often gendered and racialized workplaces. Alongside the fragmentation of claims (and conditions), there has also been a convergence on some of the meta-frames connecting health rights to labour rights.

Struggling for Social Protection

During the pandemic, protests have addressed the many inequalities that both the spread of the virus and the lockdown restrictions made ever more visible and contested. As in health movements more generally, the need to reflect on the specific impact of the health challenges on specific sections of the population has been singled out by social movement organizations, pointing to the ways in which inequalities increase the risks of infection and the effects of the virus. Building upon existing attention to intersectional inequalities, progressive social movements have addressed issues of social rights in relation to health, housing, social care and public education.

From the very beginning of the pandemic, health injustices were criticized in the many protests converging in calls for a strengthening of public welfare. While the critique of the marketization of health was raised by specific movement organizations, the Covid-19 crisis triggered protests that connected the claims of health workers with those of citizens calling for their rights as patients or as the relatives of patients to be respected. During the earliest phase of the pandemic in particular, as citizens organized to support nurses and doctors, '[w]ith this spotlight on the struggle of the health sector, organized workers in the sector were able to get ahead of the narrative and sway significant parts of the public opinion towards a stern critique of the cuts in the national health service' (Workers Inquiry Network 2020, 9). From this starting point of an expression of solidarity with workers in the health system, the public discourse often became more and more politicized, singling out the constant cuts to the welfare state as bearing broader responsibility for the spread of the virus. While the banners on balconies were initially aimed at expressing gratitude to health workers, eventually 'the slogans started to become more political and addressed many different demands and topics, from housing issues to access to basic social services' (Workers Inquiry Network 2020, 10–11).

An innovative frame, developed within feminist collectives, connected the pandemic with care and reproduction. As one activist from the Swiss Frauen*streik noted, health inequalities infringe upon human rights as

> [t]he coronavirus pandemic is a tragic reminder that the global economic system depletes our capacities for social reproduction and thus, survival. . . . COVID-19 is drawing more attention to the fact that those left furthest behind by this system are now on the front lines doing essential work that sustains livelihoods. Their health and well-being is critical to the global effort to contain this pandemic. Yet, substantial lapses in governance have undermined, for these groups especially, the rights to health, housing, food, workplace protections, and environmental justice. All of these are human rights claims, and the enjoyment of each right requires all the others. (Thieme and Tibet 2020)

According to the Italian feminist network Non Una Di Meno-Roma (2020), the frame of care has the potential to bridge various struggles by referring to 'all those activities that regenerate human life in a given historical and social formation. These include not only the reproduction of generations, the affective and bodily care of everyone, including adults, children and the elderly, but also the care of spaces and the household, education, access to culture, services, leisure and social relations'. In this frame, the pandemic is considered as being fuelled by a neoliberal model 'rooted in the celebration of the market and social competition, in individual responsibilities in adapting to risk. It has demanded the privatization and erosion of the public institutions and programmes that contributed to partially redistribute reproductive and care work in the 20th century.' Feminist activists have also denounced the ways in which the pandemic aggravated the consequences of the dismantling of the welfare state, promoting a 'feminization of work' based upon

> flexibility, total availability and the exploitation and valorization of relational, linguistic and care capacities. If, on the one hand, reproduction has become immediately productive, on the other hand, value chains feed on the exploitation of gendered, racialized and queer subjectivities, thus rendering the lives of entire generations precarious. With the outbreak of the pandemic, the fragility of the reproductive and care structures, starting from the healthcare system, has become evident. (Non Una Di Meno-Roma 2020)

An attention to care also emerged in the critique of online teaching, which is considered to be a consequence of neoliberalism, not only as a result of the budget cuts that reduced personnel and infrastructure, but also because of a distorted concept of caring, with 'platform capitalism' accused of having increased the opportunities to appropriate knowledge with 'accentuated social differences and discrimination based on ability' (Non Una Di Meno-Roma 2020). More broadly, the political consequences of online learning are stigmatized as

> [t]he transmission of knowledge cannot be separated from proximity to peers and teachers, which plays a fundamental role in building autonomous relationships, away from the family. The impossibility of proximity will have serious consequences, from an emotional and social point of view, but also from a political one: schools and universities are places where the young discover and nourish both erotic and political passions.
> (Non Una Di Meno-Roma 2020)

The pandemic also increased the impact of inequalities in housing conditions due to the fact that 'the availability of a domestic comfort zone equipped with large spaces and ICT were privileged elements limited to specific social classes' (Tassinari, Chesta and Cini 2020). This is also linked to the activists' condemnation of daily violence, harassment and other types of abuse related with gender inequalities, which had already been a target of women's movements before the pandemic. In fact, in many cases, 'the home is no refuge from a pandemic, but a place of oppression, threat, violence, even femicide' (Non Una Di Meno-Roma 2020). The fragility of marginalized groups is highlighted, as 'people who don't even live in homes face different kinds of vulnerabilities' (Paulson 2020).

In line with broader reflections, activists defined the different types of inequalities which affect the health hazards as intersectional. This has been one of the central frames connected with health injustice. May Black and colleagues have highlighted the fact that

> Black American communities have disproportionately contracted and died of the novel-coronavirus, or that around the globe, indigenous communities have contracted the virus, or that migrants, refugees and other marginalized folk are being stigmatized and unjustly discriminated against for supposedly spreading the virus, that these populations are also, disproportionately under-served or outright neglected by medical services – all is related to the systemic oppression, racism and colonial biopolitical practices that pre-figured the arrival of COVID-19. Moreover, increasing neoliberal cuts to healthcare systems as well as the constant drive towards privatization have meant that even basic healthcare is increasingly out of reach for the poor.
>
> (May Black, Chattopadhyay and Chisholm 2020)

At the peak of the protests against the murder of George Floyd in summer 2020, the Black Lives Matter campaign strongly denounced the deadly effects of ethnic inequalities, claiming that 'recent events have made it clear that being African-American in the United States or Black in Brazil, and in so many other countries with strong structural racism, also means that you belong to a high risk social group' (Bringel 2020). All around the globe, during the wave of Black Lives Matter protests in June and July 2020, a narrative of intersectionality emerged as the basis for a broad coalition, not only to address systemic racism (of different forms, not solely anti-black), but also to give voice to black people, their narratives, their positions and representation (della Porta, Lavizzari and Reiter 2022).

In general terms, frame bridging around the concept of intersectionality has made it possible to present various inequalities as being interlinked, due to the fact that the pandemic provided even more visibility to the deadly effects of social injustice. In fact, as Lesley Wood (2020a) noted,

> The virus hits institutionalized, immigrant, poorer, indigenous and racialized communities harder. Neighbourhoods where there are more longstanding health problems, more crowded housing and transportation spread the virus. Shutting things down, or forcing people to separate when some people lack access to clean water or medical help or harm reduction services, means some are sacrificed for the greater good.

Furthermore, through an intersectional feminist framing, women's struggles have been linked to social struggles, given the fact that women more commonly populate the informal labour force, as domestic workers, home carers and street food vendors, most of which were not covered by state subsides (Ventura Alfaro 2020). Various forms of collective mobilizations thus signalled a will to be 'in lockdown but not silenced' or a made a call to 'spread solidarity not the contagion', pointing to the broader context of the pandemic rather than to individual responsibility.

The pandemic could also generally be said to have made well-rooted claims advocating for public responsibility and state intervention more resonant. In their prognostic framing, activists called for 'welfare institutions to be structurally refinanced and rendered universal', 'free and supportive institutions to which everyone may have access: a public and laic healthcare system, more territorial clinics, continuous hiring and permanent contracts for staff; investment in school, training and research; childcare services; support and care for the most vulnerable; guarantee of the right to housing; social security' (Non Una Di Meno-Roma 2020). In doing so, activists also pointed to the need 'for the democratic reappropriation of social infrastructures. To defend the public means to imagine common institutions and freedom beyond the State' (Non Una Di Meno-Roma 2020). In this fashion, claims for social rights have been bridged with the idea of *commoning*, which had already been thematized by the global justice movement. This approach defines an area of activities that is not simply 'public' but rather, given its high value for human heritage, requires a status of its own that goes beyond the claim for state intervention, and establishes the right of citizens to participate in the definition of common goods (rather than just public goods). In this direction, claims for a universal basic income have been framed as care income or a quarantine income defined as, 'an income of self-determination: universal and unconditional, addressed to individuals and not to the family, not connected to work, citizenship and conditions of residence, which must guarantee economic autonomy, an instrument to escape from gender violence, from exploitation, of labour and of the ecosystem' (Non Una Di Meno-Roma 2020).

Struggling for Environmental Justice

Framing activities during the pandemic have also linked the health crisis to the environmental crisis. The connection between the two emerged first and foremost within proposals for alternative forms of production and consumption. As many local markets were shut down, collectives within the Community-Supported Agriculture (CSA) movement framed the proximity between producers and consumers as a source of healthier food, especially relevant in a moment in which the global food chain was disrupted and food prices increased. Thus, activists from cooperatives and networks of alternative producers explained that '[w]e are on the brink of a global food crisis, not because of lack of available food, but rather because it cannot be harvested or transported to consumers through the industrial long chain food system. The future genuinely lies in building stronger short food supply chains that allow local food sovereignty and traceability' (URGENCI 2020). The security of the small-scale market was thus also emphasized as security against the virus:

> [o]pen air CSA distributions of preordered and pre-paid produce from farms are one of the safest ways of providing food, safer than indoor supermarkets! . . . In the current pandemic, Community Supported Agriculture weekly share distribution has been widely maintained, thanks to the safe nature of how it is done, and the hugely responsive reaction of both producers and consumers in ensuring that it is done in accordance with new, highly rigorous health and safety regulations. CSA shares are prepared upfront. This drastically reduces human contact with the food and between people. CSA is planned in advance. There is no need to gather, queue or stand in line at a check-out like in a supermarket. Each group can organize things so that the pick-up is staggered and there are never more than a small handful of people present at any one time. There are no cash transactions: everything is ordered and paid for in advance and paid for on-line or by cheque. . . . Distribution is short and immediate. (URGENCI 2020)

Attention has also been paid to unhitching the call for degrowth from the misery caused by the pandemic. In this sense, activists struggled to keep control of more problematic narratives. Faced with misleading statements like 'mother nature is cleansing itself' or 'humanity is the virus', climate activist groups stated that 'any claim that a global pandemic and loss of thousands of human lives is a *good* thing for the climate is far more dangerous than the virus itself' (Thompson 2020). In an attempt to stress the potential for change opened up by the crisis, environmental activists maintained that,

> Contrary to claims of some critics, the ravages of COVID-19 do not represent degrowth worlds strived for by social movements. Yes, the health crisis has provoked declines in natural resources used and waste generated, giving welcome respite to ecosystems. And yes, the lives of some people have slowed down, as ambitious schedules give way to more time for reflection and relationships. But no, unevenly-suffered trauma, impoverishment, and death are not features of degrowth; on the contrary, these are precisely the kind of phenomena that planned degrowth aims to avoid. We would like to see societies slow down by design, not disaster. However, it looks like transitions away from growth may be largely unplanned and messy, in conditions not of our own choosing. Conditions like the ones we are living through now. (Paulson 2020)

In this manner, the health crisis has been framed as a discursive opportunity for the struggle against climate change. As 'a historical rupture', the moment of crisis requires a shared effort 'to reflect on how we can, from our diverse positions, face this moment, organize, and collectively imagine radical alternative modes of living: those with more time for community, relationship building, and care for each other as well as the non-human world' (Paulson 2020). In this broad perspective, some activists refer to the need for

> a spiritual or ethical reconnection with the earth, and each other. Indigenous peoples have long warned of the consequences of our alienation from the rest of nature, the penchant of modernity to think of human beings as outside of nature, somehow not bound by the limits and norms of the planet around us. In their movements they have brought back a diversity of ways of being and knowing ... buen vivir, ubuntu, sumac kawsay, kyosei, country, minobimaatasiiwin, swaraj, and many others ... that speak of living with the earth and each other in harmony. (Kothari 2020)

Struggling against State Violence and Repression

As periods of pandemic are also characterized by constraints on civil liberties and increased surveillance, activists have often targeted the harsh restrictions on freedom of movement as well as the mass deployment of the police and even of the army in order to patrol city centres and surrounding areas. While a general opposition to the lockdown has mainly been promoted by right-wing groups, progressive groups have been selectively calling for the reopening of schools and public services as well as the reestablishment of protest rights. Through the use of vehicle caravans (as in Israel) or bicycle marches (as in Slovenia), progressive groups have contested what they have seen as attempts of governments to exploit the crisis in order to limit political participation and the rights of citizens. In Hungary and Poland, protesters have expressed concerns regarding the restriction of civil liberties by right-wing populist regimes. In the United States, they have stigmatized attempts by President Donald Trump to postpone the presidential election by, among other things, launching an attack on the mail system. In countries where protesters were already highly mobilized before the onset of the pandemic, such as Chile or Lebanon, progressive social movements denounced the corruption of politics and called for transparency. More generally, as Bringel (2020) noted, protestors targeted perceived authoritarian practices, such as 'the military in the streets, states of emergency where everything was suspended and the establishment of a dangerous warlike narrative', but also 'permanent surveillance from the most classic forms to digital tracking and drones, control and management of big data, new facial recognition devices, and other sophisticated forms of social control'.

One illustration of how the lockdown conditions particularly affected the poorest segment of the population can be found in India, where activists denounced increasing levels of surveillance as well as the ban on all protests (Mallige and Thapliyal 2020). Contestation emerged especially after 24 March 2020, when Prime Minister Narendra Modi announced a three-week national lockdown, with just four hours' notice. The measures had especially dramatic effects on the tens of millions of internal and international migrants (estimated to number up to 500 million), many of whom are seasonal workers, and especially on those from impoverished Dalit, Adivasi and Muslim communities. As a consequence, '[w]hen lockdown was imposed, the vast majority of them became unemployed overnight. Shortly thereafter, they ran out of food and money to pay rent. Local authorities declared the high-density slums which most of them called home "containment zones" and placed severe and overnight restrictions on movement' (Mallige and Thapliyal 2020). In this context, migrants and racialized minorities became scapegoats for the spread of the virus.

Similarly, in Europe, in countries as diverse as Serbia, Ireland and Germany, protestors targeted the scapegoating of undocumented migrants as well as the scapegoating of those providing them with help. In addition to the militarization of borders, they denounced the sealing of overcrowded asylum and reception centres, with inmates isolated from the outside world (Milan 2020; Cox 2020). Thus, German activists claimed that '[t]he COVID-19 pandemic has laid bare some of the most endemic flaws of the shared accommodation system for refugees* in Germany. Lack of privacy, overcrowded spaces and more generally the exercise of biopower on racialized non-citizens are some among the most egregious shortcomings' (Perolini 2020). Thus, 'the COVID-19 pandemic has worsened the conditions of people on the move, stigmatized, segregated and discriminated even more than before. In the pandemic, local governments have found a justification to further restrict freedom of movement and enact the militarization of borders' (Milan 2020).

More generally speaking, there has been a condemnation of repression, and not only in authoritarian contexts. Police violence came to the fore with the global protests against the killing of the African American man George Floyd by a white policeman in Minneapolis on 25 May 2020. The campaign launched by the Black Lives Matter in the United States in the immediate aftermath of the killing spread all over the globe, condemning the racist bias in the police enforcement of public order, but also systemic racism more widely, and demanding that the police be defunded and restructured. In France, just as in other countries that were involved in the wave of global protests in 2019, the state reaction to the pandemic has been denounced as 'rooted in a context of exacerbated social conflict, in which the tensions and contradictions that cross our societies on a daily basis are increasing both rapidly and unexpectedly' (Workers Inquiry Network 2020, 14). Massive, long-lasting protests by the Yellow Vests movement, and a three-month-long general strike against the pension reform, were connected to the resistance against a 'global state of exception' (Workers Inquiry Network 2020, 15).

Aside from calling for social and environmental justice, progressive social movements that mobilized during the pandemic are demonstrating that the path to achieve these ends is not through the centralization of political decision-making, and even less so through technocratic exercises, but rather by increasing the participation of citizens. For many activists, the broad aim of their action is the development of radical conceptions and practices of democracy. Thus, as activists noted, '[w]ith the whole world listening, we have possibly history's biggest chance of changing course. We can refashion the economy and polity, local to global, to be respectful and sensitive to ecological limits, and to work for all of humanity. ... We need a dramatic transformation towards genuine democracy, a swaraj ('self-rule' in Sanskrit) that encompasses not only all humans, but the planet as a whole, based on an ethics of life' (Kothari 2020). In this direction, there has been a revival of the claim of rights to commons, defined as being so fundamental that they need to be managed through the direct participation of the citizens. As David Bollier (2020) has noted: '[t]hroughout history commoning has always been an essential survival strategy, and so it is in this crisis. When the state, market, or monarchy fail to provide for basic needs, commoners themselves usually step up to devise their own mutual aid systems.'

Framing Contention in the Pandemic: Some Conclusions

During the pandemic, progressive social movements have focussed first and foremost on social injustice, mobilizing in moral shock against the great disruption the pandemic caused in the living conditions of the poorest parts of the population. Vehicle caravans, pot banging, collective performances of protest songs from balconies, live-streamed actions, digital rallies, virtual marches, walk-outs, boycotts and rent-strikes have emerged as ways of condemning what the pandemic made all the more evident and all the less tolerable: the depth of inequality and its dramatic consequences in terms of human lives (della Porta 2020b; Martinez 2020).

In summary, it has been shown in this section how progressive movements have adapted their framing practices to adapt to the evolution of the pandemic.

On issues of workers' rights, the pandemic has seen the elaboration of an identity of precarious and invisible workers who are nonetheless capable of acquiring visibility and recognition given the centrality of their contribution to the survival of society. In terms of other sources of inequality, it has been shown how an intersectional definition of the self has been proposed in order to bridge concerns with the impact of inequality in housing, education, gender, race and age on the spread of the virus and its effects. Health rights, thus, become a sort of master frame in the calls for social justice. As justice is connected to climate change, the causes of the pandemic crisis are singled out in the environmental crisis, and ideas of proximity and respect for nature are presented as alternatives to global exploitation. With regard to repression and democracy, collective framing stigmatizes the repressive response to the pandemic in both democratic and authoritarian countries. While physical distancing, sanitation and even lockdown measures are considered to be justified at times by the need to protect the weakest sections of the population, there is criticism of the top-down imposition of these rules, the lack of transparency and the increasing centralization of decisions, with consequent restrictions on the right to protest. In contrast, the deepening of democracy, through the empowerment of citizens, is considered to be essential in fighting the pandemic.

Since March 2020, workers have mobilized all over the world in defence of labour rights that they perceive to be under threat. Both factory workers and white collar workers in essential sectors called for strikes, demanding personal protective equipment and sanitized environments. Workers in the so-called gig economy, including delivery riders, Amazon drivers and call centre workers, mobilized in wildcat strikes, walked out of workplaces, called in sick and staged flashmobs to demand protection against infection as well as a broader range of labour rights (Tassinari, Chesta and Cini 2020). Workers who became unemployed during the pandemic – from those involved in the tourism sector to those working in cultural and artistic activities – also mobilized to demand income support. In many cases they also shone a light on the attempts made by their companies to discourage collective action by firing those who stood up to condemn the lack of safety conditions.

In most of the countries that have been hardest hit by the pandemic there were also calls for social rights, primarily related to public health, but also to social services, housing and public education. Workers in the healthcare sector called not only for the immediate provision of life-saving devices but also for resources to be invested into the public provision of health. Throughout the world, healthcare personnel in private hospitals staged (socially distanced) stay-ins to protest against the deterioration of their working conditions, the underfunding of the public health system and low salaries. Inequalities have also been challenged by students, who called for reductions in fees and an increase in grants. Rent strikes spread, as the loss of jobs made it more and more difficult to pay increasingly high rents. Feminist groups denounced the fact that the increased burden of care work had fallen particularly hard on women, given the shutting down of schools and social services. Within a frame of environmental justice, protests also addressed the increasing deterioration of nature and the effects that this has had on the spread and lethality of the pandemic itself.

While progressive movements gave priority to the defence of social rights, concerns also emerged with regard to civil and political rights. The pandemic has been a time in which the poor, migrants and homeless people have been variously accused of spreading the virus. It has been a period characterized by a lack of transparency and low accountability, given the proclamation of states of emergency, which have also been used – at different times and to different degrees – to curb dissent. Xenophobic governments have increased forced repatriation and closed their borders, going as far as refusing to accept refugees. Even in less dramatic cases, the mass media has mainly focussed on the pandemic to the exclusion of other pressing concerns, often with the result of simply promoting fear. Progressive social movements have opposed these trends. Faced with decreasing transparency and increasing repression during and after the lockdown, activists have called the political and economic powers to account through the painstaking work of collecting, elaborating and transmitting information on the effects that the pandemic has had on the poorest and most disadvantaged groups of citizens – such as prisoners, migrants and the homeless – but also on the unequal distribution of care activities within the family and violence against women.

5 Social Movements in the Pandemic: Some Conclusions

As the first genuinely global pandemic, the Covid-19 crisis has been defined as a global event, with effects stretching across the globe. It did, however, have quite different and very localized characteristics (Bringel and Pleyer 2020; Sousa 2020). Expectations about the outcomes of the pandemic from within the social sciences vary widely, from immobility to radical change, between everything going back to normal and nothing ever being the same again. According to Delanty (2021, 18), for instance, '[a]ll the evidence seems to suggest that the pandemic does not mark the transition to a new era but confirms and solidifies changes that have already occurred'. Other scholars believe instead that 'the pandemic is not a parenthesis. It is a transition point that indicates a rupture' (Vanderberghe and Véran 2021, 185). Those pointing to the potential for critical turning points have suggested that the pandemic 'has made a big dent in the

already weakened ideology that the "competitive society" does not need security and protection' (Avlijaš 2021, 240; see also Walby 2021).

While the Covid-19 pandemic is a unique historical event, this Element has
suggested that social science analyses can build on knowledge that has been
accumulated on similar classes of events, including other health catastrophes,
as well as exceptionally disruptive events such as natural disasters and wars.
By combining insights from this stream of literature, I have singled out both
challenges and opportunities for progressive social movements – and progressive politics more generally – in emergency-related critical junctures.
Looking at repertoires of collective action, organizational models and framing, I have shown that innovations have built upon existing trends, developed
in responses to other crises, such as the Great Recession at the turn of the
2010s.

During the pandemic crisis, progressive social movements had to face
challenges in terms of increasing social injustice and rampant poverty, as the
spread of the virus made the deadly effects of inequalities unmistakably
evident. Increased diffusion and mortality rates were linked to a lack of health
insurance, sick leave, unemployment benefits or savings, as well as to
crowded and polluted living conditions. There was a high risk of stigmatiza-
tion of marginalized groups, such as migrants, ethnic minorities or the young.
States of emergency also brought about increasing repression, with
unaccountable emergency powers, limitations on freedom and the centralization of political power.

However, I have also argued that the pandemic crisis has created opportunities for progressive movements, such as discursive openings on issues of social
justice, an increase in public intervention, innovative forms of participation, the
building of alternative public spheres, the growth of grassroots solidarity, the
broadening of collective identification and an intensification of global connections. As with the aftermath of Hurricane Katrina in the United States, or other
extreme weather crises, during the pandemic there has also been a recognition
of the impact of social injustice, which pushes people to act in solidarity with
others and even to politicize their claims.

Challenges and opportunities are influenced by the very characteristics as
well as by the dynamics of the emergency-driven critical juncture. The social
construction of the virus is linked to broader transformations in capitalism, its
political context and in the societal resistance to it. The response of progressive
movements to the pandemic builds upon a return of the social question that was
nurtured by the global justice movement at the beginning of the millennium and
later by the anti-austerity protests that peaked in the 2010s, to then be taken up
once again during the fast spreading wave of protests that, from Lebanon to

Chile, mobilized globally in the hot autumn of 2019, reaching their height just before the official declaration of the pandemic by the WHO (della Porta 2020d). During the pandemic, progressive social movements mobilized against increasing inequalities with claims for a broadening of citizens' rights. We have seen how they staged collective actions in the streets, when possible, as well as in their workplaces, demanding a broadening of social rights, including health, work, housing, social services and education. Activists refused to pay rent and used balconies to call for health justice. They organized mutual aid initiatives in solidarity with their neighbours, but also with those most hard-hit by the pandemic and the measures introduced to contain it, offering food and shelter, medicines and legal aid. Progressive movements have also been an important source of alternative information, denouncing the dramatic effects of class, gender, generational and ethnic inequalities. Although they have by and large considered the restriction of individual freedoms as justified in the name of solidarity, progressive social movements have also mobilized against the repression of activism and violence against the most marginalized groups of the population, demanding transparency and accountability

In summary, the pandemic has demonstrated the potential of periods of deep crisis to intensify the debate on broad transformations. As the pandemic changed everyday life, progressive social movements created much-needed spaces for reflection on the post-pandemic world, which is conceived as a break with the pre-pandemic status quo. By building alternative public spheres, they have articulated demands for radical change. Indeed, activists have produced lay knowledge that is at least as valuable as the specialized knowledge of experts. It has been noted that

> [e]verywhere, there is evidence that people are rethinking and imagining things like alternatives to our outmoded educational systems, an economy that works for all to meet real, basic needs, a new and better kind of politics for the purpose of radical social transformation, the shifts in culture and affect to design the whole ways of life we desire, the fair, ambitious, and binding global approach that the unfolding climate change will force on states and other elite institutions. (Foran 2020)

There are therefore expectations that the mobilization against the pandemic might have opened a discursive space for deep transformations. As indicated by previous research, the expansion of citizenship rights after disasters is, however, a possible but not necessary outcome. Its achievement requires in fact that the citizens mobilize in order to reduce the power of elites and/or push them towards compromise (Kier and Krebs 2020; Starr 2010). Furthermore, whether the outcome of the crisis will be a garrison state or an expansion of deliberative democracy, as happened following Typhoon Hiyan in the Philippines (Curato 2020), is an open question for future studies. Indeed, it is still to be seen what the long-term capacity of progressive movements is to consolidate some contingent victories in terms of not only more protection at work but also investment in public health, and more state intervention in social protection in general. While discursive opportunities have emerged for those concerned with social justice, powerful interests have also been strengthened by this crisis, as testified for by the increasing fortunes of selected economic elites. There are, moreover, many issues open for progressive social movements in their attempts to build solidarity in what is a very difficult time.

Firstly, the pandemic has impacted upon an already fragmented class structure, introducing new sources of inequality between those who work in a safe environment (or even from home) and those who are instead either occupied in essential services with limited health protection or have lost their precarious jobs due to the crisis. Even within each of these groups, there are differences in terms not only of the degree of job insecurity but also of gender discrimination in the way in which the activities of caring for young or disabled persons, which increased during the pandemic, are distributed. Among those who work in essential services, divisions have emerged between those who have more labour rights (and can strike or threaten to strike) and the growing precariat, who do not possess stable contracts and at times are even considered to be independent workers. The pandemic not only increased inequalities, but also the fragmentation of the interests and positions as it produces effects that are specific for different groups and in different territories. As Claus Offe (2021) has noted, the position of each individual in relation to the virus varies with the specific risks vis-à-vis both the health hazard and the effects of lockdown measures on individual socio-economic conditions. Thus, 'for a moment, there was a sense of interdependency and unity. However, after a few weeks of lockdown, the unity started to fracture' (Vanderberghe and Véran 2021, 181).

The pandemic also made the inequalities in the endowment of social rights more visible: from the very right to health coverage and sick leave (or leave to care for others who are sick) to the right to housing and access to public education or social services. The orders to shelter-in-place increased the impact of unequal living conditions in relation to housing rights, discriminating against those who have insufficient or no private space and no access to ever more important equipment such as computers and connected devices. The pandemic has especially disrupted the most commodified educational systems, with dramatic consequences for students, teachers and other workers in various roles. Also in this case, inequalities in terms of class, generation, gender and ethnic background tend to add up, leading to a growing number of citizens being driven into precarious positions. This is especially true in democracies with a residual welfare state, such as the United States, where losing one's job often implies losing one's health insurance, income and housing.

This fragmentation might also be reflected in competing demands, such as those in secure employment positions calling for lockdown measures and those in insecure employment positions fearing the potential consequences of such measures, with the former often more vocal than the latter. As demonstrated by the Black Lives Matter protests, when stratified inequalities become more visible, specific triggers, such as episodes of police violence on ethnic minorities, can provide a symbolic catalyst for the convergence of different struggles. Even if there have been examples of convergences on shared demands for public health, workers' rights, a basic income and universal welfare, there is also evidence of the difficulty of overcoming intersectional divisions and mobilizing on a common platform.

Progressive social movements are also required to mobilize under very limiting circumstances. As mentioned in this Element, protests on the Left have contested authoritarian measures in Israel, Slovenia and Hungary, whose governments have been accused of exploiting the health crisis to centralize power and repress the opposition. More sporadically, activists have denounced an instrumental and biased use of restrictive measures to selectively repress protests on issues such as migrants' rights or the rights of sex-workers. By and large, however, lockdown and hygiene measures (such as the wearing of masks) have been contested on the Right, while the Left counter-mobilized in defence of what they define as measures of solidarity with the weakest sections of the population. Furthermore, workers in those sectors most hit by the restrictions have preferred to claim public subsidies than call for reopening. While up to now, progressive social movements in democratic contexts have addressed social rights more than civil liberties, they have, however, also denounced the effects of the state of emergency on the very right to protest. This has been the case not only in countries where democracy was already considered to be at risk, but also in the case of movements mobilizing the most powerless groups in the population, such as migrants, the homeless and prisoners. The Black Lives Matter protests pointed to police violence against racialized people; feminist groups denounced societal violence against women.

It should be noted that it is still difficult to organize effective protests. Even after the end of lockdown, restrictions on street-based actions are still in place and can be used arbitrarily to repress contentious politics. Online activities selectively involve the most connected, excluding the voice of the most powerless. The new mutualism brings about the challenge, already singled out in other emergencies, of having to invest limited resources to offer surrogate services to substitute insufficient state provisions. In addition, there is an increase in frustration, given the scarce capacity to address fast-growing needs as well as the insufficient availability of the professional skills among the volunteers. On a collective level, there is a risk of de-politicization, while burnout is considered a significant problem on the individual level. At the same time, the power dynamics between those who help and those who are helped are difficult to keep in check.

The crisis has also deeply challenged public institutions, in both democratic and non-democratic contexts. This is particularly the case on issues of legitimacy and efficacy (Offe 2021) on which the debate within progressive movements is still ongoing. Something that has been highlighted by the pandemic and has yet to be addressed is the question of the democratic accountability of experts and the role of science itself. Indeed, the relationship between politics and science has been shown to be problematic, as the very gesture of political institutions to abide by scientific knowledge resulted in science becoming politicized. In a situation characterized by such high levels of uncertainty, with scientific evidence still under development on the most critical issues related to the prevention and the cure of Covid-19, references to scientific evidence have multiplied. This brought about warnings about the danger of techno-populism, as political battles have developed upon the use of politicized expertise to propose alternative scientific truths (Zielonka 2021, 66). The simplification of the public debate on science may endanger the image of science as plural, free and non-dogmatic, with the recognition of the legitimacy of different positions by medical doctors, according to scientific branches, theoretical schools and methodological choices (Zielonka 2021, 61).

In conclusion, while it is too early to assess the outcomes of these struggles, their very existence confirms the important role progressive social movements can play in critical junctures, including during an emergency such as a pandemic crisis. In action, different (pre-existing and emerging) groups are building ties and bridging frames. These energies are connecting around a series of central challenges for the construction of post-pandemic alternatives. Most importantly, progressive movements are elaborating innovative ideas about how to contrast ever-growing inequalities in labour conditions and income, but also between generations, genders, ethnic groups and different states. Here the proposed alternatives are not only a return of the labour rights that neoliberal capitalism had already taken away, with consequences that have become all the more stark during the pandemic, but also the development of claims for a basic income for those who are expelled from or have never entered the labour market, as well as for rights to education, housing and public health. In performing these activities, progressive social movements constitute public spheres in which participation is praised in a vision of solidarity as something that is born out of a recreated sense of shared destiny. Indeed, democracy can be said to have been enhanced by the very presence of these voices in the public debate.

References

All entries from *Interface* are available online at www.interfacejournal.net/inter face-volume-12-issue-1/. All entries from the the volume *Alerta Global* are available online at http://biblioteca.clacso.edu.ar/clacso/se/20200826014541/ Alerta-global.pdf.

Abers, R., Von Bulow, M., and Rossi, F. (2021). State–Society Relations in Uncertain Times: Social Movement Strategies, Ideational Contestation and the Pandemic in Brazil and Argentina. *International Political Science Review*, 42(3), 333–49.

Acciari, L. (2020). Domestic Workers' Struggles in Times of Pandemic Crisis. *Interface: A Journal for and about Social Movements*, 21(1), 121–7.

Alexander, K. (2020). Hambre, ira y un nuevo movimiento social en Sudáfrica. In B. Bringel and G. Pleyers (eds.), *Alerta Global*. Buenos Aires: Clacso, 229–40.

Allen, A. (2016). *The End of Progress: Decolonizing the Normative Foundations of Critical Theory*. New York: Columbia University Press.

Aronis, C. (2009). The Balconies of Tel-Aviv: Cultural History and Urban Politics. *Israel Studies*, 14(3), 157–80.

Avlijaš, S. (2021). Security for Whom? Inequality and Human Dignity in Times of the Pandemic. In G. Delanty (ed.), *Pandemics, Politics and Society*. Berlin: De Gruyter, 227–42.

Azmanova, A. (2021). Battlegrounds of Justice: The Pandemic and What Really Grieves the 99%. In G. Delanty (ed.), *Pandemics, Politics and Society*. Berlin: De Gruyter, 243–55.

Baldwin, R. (2005). *Democracy and Diseases*. Berkeley: University of California Press.

Banaszak-Holl, J. C., Levitsky, S. R., and Zald M. N. (eds.) (2010). *Social Movements and the Transformation of American Health Care*. Oxford: Oxford University Press.

Banerjee. S. (2020). Espacios comunitarios en la India: ¿construyendo solidaridad en tiempos de pandemia? In B. Bringel and G. Pleyers (eds.), *Alerta Global*. Buenos Aires: Clacso, 141–50.

Bao, H. (2020). 'Anti-Domestic Violence Little Vaccine': A Wuhan-Based Feminist Activist Campaign during COVID-19. *Interface: A Journal for and about Social Movements*, 21(1), 53–63.

Beissinger, M. R. (2002). *Nationalist Mobilization and the Collapse of the Soviet State*. Cambridge: Cambridge University Press.

Blee, K. (2012). *Democracy in the Making: How Activists Groups Form.* Oxford: Oxford University Press.

Bollier, D. (2020). Commoning as a Pandemic Survival Strategy. Free, Fair and Alive. https://freefairandalive.org/commoning-as-a-pandemic-survival-strategy/

Bosi, L., and Zamponi, L. (2019). *Resistere alla crisi.* Bologna: Il Mulino.

Bringel, B. (2020). Covid-19 and the New Global Chaos. *Interface: A Journal for and about Social Movements,* 21(1), 392–9.

Bringel, B., and Pleyers, G. (2020) Introducion: La pandemia y el suo eco global. In B. Bringel and G. Pleyers (eds.), *Alerta Global.* Buenos Aires: Clacso, 9–33.

Calvo, K., and Bejarano, E. (2020). Music, Solidarities and Balconies in Spain. *Interface: A Journal for and about Social Movements,* 21(1), 326–32.

Castells, M. (2020). Reset. In B. Bringel and G. Pleyers (eds.), *Alerta Global.* Buenos Aires: Clacso, 101–6.

Chan, C., and Tsui, A. (2020). Hong Kong: de las protestas democráticas a la huelga de trabajadores médicos en la pandemia. In B. Bringel and G. Pleyers (eds.), *Alerta Global.* Buenos Aires: Clacso, 152–9.

Chattopadhyay, S., Wood, L., and Cox, L. (2020). Organizing amidst Covid-19. *Interface: A Journal for and about Social Movements,* 21(1), 1–9.

Chernilo, D. (2021). Another Globalization: Covid-19 and the Cosmopolitan Imagination. In G. Delanty (ed.), *Pandemics, Politics and Society.* Berlin: De Gruyter, 157–70.

Clemens, E. S., and Minkoff, D. C. (2007). Beyond the Iron Law. In D. A. Snow, S. H. Soule and H. Kriesi, (eds.), *The Blackwell Companion to Social Movements.* Oxford: Blackwell, 155–70.

Collier, D. and Munck, G. L. (2017). Building Blocks and Methodological Challenges: A Framework for Studying Critical Junctures. *Qualitative and Multi-Method Research,* 15(1), 2–8.

Cox, L. (2020). Forms of Social Movement in the Crisis: A View from Ireland. *Interface: A Journal for and about Social Movements,* 21(1), 22–33.

Crossley, N. (2006). *Contesting Psychiatry.* London: Routledge.

Curato, N. (2020). *Democracy in Times of Misery.* Oxford: Oxford University Press.

Delanty, G. (2021). Introduction: The Pandemic in Historical and Global Context. In G. Delanty (ed.), *Pandemics, Politics and Society.* Berlin: De Gruyter, 1–23.

della Porta, D. (1995). *Social Movements, Political Violence, and the State.* Cambridge: Cambridge University Press.

della Porta, D. (2008). Comparative Analysis. In D. della Porta and M. Keating (eds.), *Approaches and Methodologies in the Social Sciences*. Cambridge: Cambridge University Press, 198–222.

della Porta, D. (ed.) (2009). *Democracy in Social Movements*. London: Palgrave.

della Porta, D. (2012). Comparative analysis. In D. della Porta and M. Keating (eds.), *Approaches and Methodological in the Social Sciences*. Cambridge: Cambridge University Press, 198–222.

della Porta, D. (2013). *Can Democracy Be Saved?* Cambridge: Polity Press.

della Porta, D. (2015). *Social Movements in Times of Austerity*. Cambridge: Polity Press.

della Porta, D. (2017) *Where did the Revolution Go?* Cambridge: Cambridge University Press.

della Porta, D. (2020a). *How Social Movements Can Save Democacy*. Cambridge: Polity.

della Porta, D. (2020b). Movimientos sociales en tiempos de COVID-19: Otro mundo es necesario. In B. Bringel and G. Pleyers (eds.), *El mundo en suspenso*. Buenos Aires: Clacso, 55–62.

della Porta, D. (2020c). How Progressive Social Movements Can Save Democracy in Pandemic Times. *Interface: A Journal for and about Social Movements*, 12(1), 355–8.

Della Porta D. (2020d). Spreading Protests: Changing Paths of Transnationalization of Social Movements. *Alternate Routes: A Journal of Critical Social Research*, 31(1), 116–34.

della Porta, D. (2021). Progressive Social Movements, Democracy and the Pandemic. In G. Delanty (ed.), *Pandemics, Politics and Society*. Berlin: De Gruyter, 209–26.

della Porta, D., and Diani, M. (2020). *Social Movements: An Introduction*, 3rd ed. Oxford: Blackwell.

della Porta, D., and Mattoni, A. (eds.) (2014). *Spreading Protest: Social Movements in Times of Crisis*. Colchester: ECPR Press.

della Porta, D., and Pavan, E. (2017) Repertoires of Knowledge Practices: Social Movements in Times of Crisis. *Qualitative Research in Organizations and Management: An International Journal*, 12 (4), 297–314.

della Porta, D., and Rucht, D. (1995). Social Movement Sectors in Context: A Comparison of Italy and West Germany, 1965–1990. In J. C. Jenkins and B. Klandermans (eds.), *The Politics of Social Protest*. Minneapolis: Minnesota University Press, 299–72.

della Porta, D., and Steinhilper, E. (2021). *Contentious Migrant Solidarity Book: Shrinking Spaces and Civil Society Contestation*. London: Routledge.

della Porta, D., Lavizzari, A., and Reiter, H. (2022), The Spreading of the Black Lives Matter Movement Campaign: The Italian Case in Cross-National Perspective. *Sociological Forum*. https://doi.org/10.1111/socf.12818.

Diesner, D. (2020). Self-Governance Food System before and during the Covid-Crisis on the Example of CampiAperti, Bologna. *Interface: A Journal for and about Social Movements*, 21(1), 266–73.

Duke, B. (2020). The Effects of the COVID-19 Crisis on the Gig Economy and Zero Hour Contracts. *Interface: A Journal for and about Social Movements*, 21(1), 115–20.

Duyvendak, J. W., and Jasper, J. M. (eds). (2015). *Breaking Down the State: Protestors Engaged*. Amsterdam: Amsterdam University Press.

Dynes, R. L., and Quarantelli, E. Q. (1977). *Helping Behavior in Large Scale Disasters*. University of Delaware, Disaster Research Center, preliminary paper #48.

Epstein, S. (1996). *Impure Science*. Berkeley: University of California Press.

Epstein, S. (2010). The Strength of Diverse Time. In J. C. Banaszak-Holl, S. R. Levitsky and M. N. Zald (eds.), *Social Movements and the Transformation of American Health Care*. Oxford: Oxford University Press, 79–99.

Escobar, A. (2020). Transiciones post-pandemia en clave civilizatoria. In B. Bringel and G. Pleyers (eds.), *Alerta Global*. Buenos Aires: Clacso, 313–26.

FASE Rio de Janeiro. (2020). La pandemia desde las favelas: desigualdades e injusticias en Río de Janeiro. In B. Bringel and G. Pleyers (eds.), *Alerta Global*. Buenos Aires: Clacso, 123–32.

Fiedlschuster, M., and Reichle, L. R. (2020). Solidarity Forever? Performing Mutual Aid in Leipzig, Germany. *Interface: A Journal for and about Social Movements*, 21(1), 317–25.

Fligstein, N., and McAdam, D. (2012). *A Theory of Fields*. Oxford: Oxford University Press.

Foran, J. (2020). Eco Vista in the Quintuple Crisis. *Interface: A Journal for and about Social Movements*, 21(1), 284–91.

Frickel, S. (2010). Shadow Mobilization for Environmental Health and Justice. In J. C. Banaszak-Holl, S. R. Levitsky and M. N. Zald (eds.), *Social Movements and the Transformation of American Health Care*. Oxford: Oxford University Press, 171–87.

Gamson, W. (2013). Injustice Frames. In D. Snow, D. della Porta, B. Klandermans and D. McAdam (eds.), *Blackwell Encyclopedia on Social and Political Movements*. Oxford: Blackwell, 607–8.

Gamson, W., Fireman, B., and Rytina, S. (1982). *Encounters with Unjust Authority*. Homewood: Dorsey Press.

Gerbaudo, P. (2020). Clapforcarers: la solidaridad de base frente al coronavirus. In B. Bringel and G. Pleyers (eds.), *Alerta Global*. Buenos Aires: Clacso, 199–204.

Gkougki, J. (2020). Corona-Crisis Affects Small Greek Farmers Who Counterstrike with a Nationwide Social Media Campaign to Unite Producers and Consumers on Local Level! *Interface: A Journal for and about Social Movements*, 21(1), 280–3.

Gravante, T., and Poma, A. (2020). Romper con el narcisismo: Emociones y activismo de base durante la pandemia. In B. Bringel and G. Pleyers (eds.), *Alerta Global*. Buenos Aires: Clacso, 128–34.

Gutierrez, F. (2020). Solidaridad y participación en una sociedad desigual: la Covid-19 en Filipinas. In B. Bringel and G. Pleyers (eds.), *Alerta Global*. Buenos Aires: Clacso, 133–40.

Hay, C. (2008) Constructivist Institutionalism. In R. A. W. Rhodes, S. A. Binder and B. A, Rockman (eds.), *The Oxford Handbook of Political Institutions*. Oxford: Oxford University Press, 56–74.

Horn, E. (2021). Tipping Points: The Anthropocene and Covid-19. In G. Delanty (ed.), *Pandemics, Politics and Society*. Berlin: De Gruyter, 123–38.

Human Rights Watch (2020). *Human Rights Dimensions of COVID-19 Response*. New York: Human Rights Watch. www.hrw.org/news/2020/03/ 19/human-rights-dimensions-covid-19-response, Accessed May 2020

International Crisis Group (2020). COVID-19 and Conflict: Seven Trends to Watch. Crisis Group Special Briefing No 4. https://d2071andvip0wj .cloudfront.net/B004-covid-19-seven-trends_0.pdf.

Ibarra, P. (2020). Movimientos sociales, cambio cultural e impactos de la pandemia. In B. Bringel and G. Pleyers (eds.), *Alerta Global*. Buenos Aires: Clacso, 343–52.

Innerarity, D. (2021). Political Decision-Making in a Pandemic. In G. Delanty (ed.), *Pandemics, Politics and Society*. Berlin: De Gruyter, 93–105.

Isin, E. F., and Nielsen, G. M. (eds.) (2008). *Acts of Citizenship*. London: Palgrave Macmillan.

Jasper, J. M. (1997). *The Art of Moral Protest: Culture, Biography and Creativity in Social Movements*. Chicago: University of Chicago Press.

Jenkins, J. (2007). Baptism of Fire: New Brunswick's Public Health Movement and the 1918 Influenza Epidemic. *Canadian Bullettin of Medical History*, 24(2), 317–42.

Johnston, H. (2018). The Revenge of Turner and Killian: Paradigm, State, and Repertoire in Social Movement Research. Paper presented at the conference

1968: 50 Years After. Florence, Cosmos, Scuola Normale Superiore, May 26–28.

Kassir, A. (2020). Líbano: Una revolución en tiempos de pandemia. In B. Bringel and G. Pleyers (eds.), *Alerta Global*. Buenos Aires: Clacso, 160–7.

Kaufman, R. R. (2017). Latin America in the Twenty-First Century. *Qualitative and Multi-Method Research*, 15(1), 16–18.

Kavada, A. (2020). Creating a Hyperlocal Infrastructure of Care: COVID-19 Mutual Aid Groups. *ISA47, Open Movements – ISA 47 Open Democracy*. www.opendemocracy.net/en/openmovements/creating-hyperlocal-infrastruc ture-care-covid-19-mutual-aid-groups.

Kerbo, H. R. (1982). Movements of 'Crisis' and Movements of 'Affluence': A Critique of Deprivation and Resource Mobilization Theory. *Journal of Conflict Resolution*, 26, 645–63.

Kier, E., and Krebs, R. (eds.) (2020). *In War's Wake*. Cambridge: Cambridge University Press.

Klandermans, B. (2013a). Frustration-Aggression. In D. Snow, D. della Porta, B. Klandermans and D. McAdam (eds.), *Blackwell Encyclopedia on Social and Political Movements*. Oxford: Blackwell, 493–4.

Klandermans, B. (2013b). The Dynamics of Demand. In J. van Stekelenburg, C. Roggeband and B. Klandermans (eds.), *The Future of Social Movement Research. Dynamics, Mechanisms, and Processes*. Minneapolis: University of Minnesota Press, 3–16.

Kleres, J. (2018). *The Social Organization of Disease*. London: Routledge.

Kothari, A. (2020). Corona Can't Save the Planet, But We Can, if We Listen to Ordinary People. *Interface: A Journal for and about Social Movements*, 21(1), 258–65.

Kothari, A., Escobar, A., Salleh, A., Demaria, F., and Acosta, A. (2020). Can the Coronavirus Save the Planet? *Open Democracy*. www.opendemocracy.net/ en/oureconomy/can-coronavirussave-planet.

Kreuder-Sonnen, C. (2019). *Emergency Powers of International Organizations*. Oxford: Oxford University Press.

Krinsky, J., and Caldwell, H. (2020). New York City's Movement Networks: Resilience, Reworking, and Resistance in a Time of Distancing and Brutality. *Open Movements – ISA 47 Open Democracy*. www.opendemocracy.net/en/ democraciaabierta/new-york-citys-movement-networksresilience-rework ing-and-resistance-in-a-time-of-distancing-and-brutality.

Landry, J., Smith, A., Agwenjang, P., Akakpo, B., Basnet, J., Chapagain, B., Gebremichael, A. Maigari, B. and Saka, N. (2020). Social Justice Snapshots: Governance Adaptations, Innovations and Practitioner Learning in a Time of

COVID-19. *Interface: A Journal for and about Social Movements*, 21(1), 371–82.

Levitsky S. R., and Banaszak-Holl, J. C. (2010). Social Movements and the Transformation of American Health Care: Introduction. In J. C. Banaszak-Holl, S. R. Levitsky and M.-N. Zald (eds.), *Social Movements and the Transformation of American Health Care*. Oxford: Oxford University Press, 3–21.

Mallige, S., and Thapliyal, N. (2020). Migrant Labourers, Covid-19 and Working-Class Struggle in the Time of Pandemic: A Report from Karnataka, India. *Interface: A Journal for and about Social Movements*, 21(1), 164–81.

Marshall, T. H. (1992). Citizenship and Social Class. In T .H. Marshall and H. D. Bottomore, *Citizens and Social Class*. London: Pluto, 3–51.

Martinez, M. (2020) Mutating Mobilizations during the Pandemic Crisis in Spain. *Interface: A Journal for and about Social Movements*, 12(1), 15–21.

Massarenti, M. (2020). How Covid-19 Led to a #Rentstrike and What It Can Teach Us about Online Organizing. *Interface: A Journal for and about Social Movements*, 21(1), 339–46.

May Black, J., Chattopadhyay, J., and Chisholm, R. (2020). Solidarity in Times of Social Distancing: Migrants, Mutual Aid, and COVID-19. *Interface: A Journal for and About Social Movements*, 21(1), 182–93.

McAdam, D., and Sewell, W. H. (2001). It's about Time: Temporality in the Study of Social Movements and Revolutions. In R. R. Aminzade, J. A. Goldstone, D. McAdam, E. J. Perry, W. H. Sewell Jr., S. Tarrow, and C. Tilly (eds.), *Silence and Voice in the Study of Contentious Politics*. New York: Cambridge University Press, 89–125.

McNeill, W. H. (1998). *Plagues and Peoples*. New York: Anchor Books

Melucci, A. (1996). *Challenging Codes*. Cambridge: Cambridge University Press.

Meyer, D., and Tarrow, S. (eds.) (2019). *The Resistance*. Oxford: Oxford University Press.

Milan, C. (2020). Refugee Solidarity along the Western Balkans Route: New Challenges and a Change of Strategy in Times of COVID-19. *Interface: A Journal for and about Social Movements*, 21(1), 208–12.

Mohanty, S. (2020). From Communal Violence to Lockdown Hunger: Emergency Responses by Civil Society Networks in Delhi, India. *Interface: A Journal for and about Social Movements*, 21(1), 47–52.

Morlino, L. (2012). *Changes for Democracy*. Oxford: Oxford University Press.

Morse, S. (ed.) (1993). *Emerging Viruses*. Oxford: Oxford University Press.

Non Una Di Meno Roma (2020). Life beyond the Pandemic. *Interface: A Journal for and About Social Movements*, 21(1), 109–14.

Nowotny, H. (2021). In AI We Trust: How the COVID-19 Pandemic Pushes us Deeper into Digitalization. In G. Delanty (ed.), *Pandemics, Politics and Society*. Berlin: De Gruyter, 107–22.

O'Donnel, G., and P. Schmitter (1986). *Transitions from Authoritarian Rule*. Baltimore: Johns Hopkins University Press.

Offe, C. (2011). What, if Anything, May We Mean by 'Progressive' Politics Today? *Trends in Social Cohesion*, 22, 79–92.

Offe, C. (2021). Corona Pandemic Policy: Exploratory Notes on Its 'Epistemic Regime'. In G. Delanty (ed.), *Pandemics, Politics and Society*. Berlin: De Gruyter, 25–42.

Paulson, S. (2020). Degrowth and Feminisms Ally to Forge Care-Full Paths Beyond Pandemic. *Interface: A Journal for and About Social Movements*, 21(1), 232–46.

Perolini, M. (2020). Abolish All Camps in Times of Corona: The Struggle Against Shared Accommodation for Refugees* in Berlin. *Interface: A Journal for and About Social Movements*, 21(1), 213–24.

Petitjean, C. (2020). El movimiento de la huelga en Francia. In B. Bringel and G. Pleyers (eds.), *Alerta Global*. Buenos Aires: Clacso, 279–87.

Pirate Care Syllabus (n.d.). Organising a Solidarity Kitchen. Pirate Care Syllabus. https://syllabus.pirate.care/session/solidaritykitchen.

Piven, F. F., and Cloward, R. A. (1977). *Poor Peoples' Movements*. New York: Pantheon

Piven, F. F., and Cloward, R. A. (1992). Normalizing Collective Protest. In A. Morris and C. McClurg Mueller (eds.), *Frontiers in Social Movement Theory*. New Haven: Yale University Press, 301–25.

Pleyers, G. (2020). Echar raiz: futuros alternativos. In B. Bringel and G. Pleyers (eds.), *Alerta Global*. Buenos Aires: Clacso, 301–12

Polanyi, K. (1957). *The Great Transformation: The Political and Economic Origins of Our Time*. London: Beacon Press.

Purkayastha, B. (2020). Divided We Stand: The Pandemic in the US. Open Movements. *ISA 47 Open Democracy*. www.opendemocracy.net/en/open movements/divided-we-stand-thepandemic-in-the-us.

Rao, H. G., and. Greve, H. R. (2018). Disaster and Community Resilience. Spanish Flu and the Formation of Retail Cooperatives in Norway. *Academy of Management Journal*, 61(1), 5–25.

Roberts, K. M. (2015). *Changing Courses: Party Systems in Latin America's Neoliberal Era*. Cambridge: Cambridge University Press.

Rosenberg, C. (1989). What is an Epidemic? Aids in Historical Perspective. *Dedalus*, 144, 1–17.

Ruiz Cayuela, S. (2020). Organising a Solidarity Kitchen: Reflections from Cooperation Birmingham. *Interface: A Journal for and about Social Movements*, 21(1), 304–9.

Sagot, M. M. (2020). Muerte, control social y bienestar en tiempos de Covid-19. In B. Bringel and G. Pleyers (eds.), *Alerta Global*. Buenos Aires: Clacso, 107–14.

Scheppele, K. L. (2005–6). Small Emergencies. *Georgia Law Review*, 40, 835–62.

Scheppele, K. L. (2010). Exceptions that Prove the Rule: Embedding Emergency Government in Everyday Constitutional Life. In S. Macedo and J. Tulis (eds.), *The Limits of Constitutional Democracy*. Princeton: Princeton University Press, 124–54.

Sewell, W. H. (1996). Three Temporalities: Toward an Eventful Sociology. In T. J. McDonald (ed.), *The Historic Turn in the Human Sciences*. Ann Arbor: University of Michigan Press, 245–80.

Sharkawi, T., and Ali, N. (2020). Acts of Whistleblowing: The Case of Collective Claim Making by Healthcare Workers in Egypt. *Interface: A Journal for and about Social Movements*, 21(1), 139–63.

Sirimane, M., and Thapliyal, N. (2020). Migrant Labourers, Covid-19 and Working-Class Struggle in the Time of Pandemic: A Report from Karnataka, India. *Interface: A Journal for and about Social Movements*, 21(1), 164–81.

Smith, J. (2020). Responding to Coronavirus Pandemic: Human Rights Movement-Building to Transform Global Capitalism. *Interface: A Journal for and about Social Movements*, 21(1), 359–66.

Smucker, J. M. (2014). Can Prefigurative Politics Replace Political Strategy? *Berkeley Journal of Sociology*, 58, 74–82.

Snow, D. A., and Lessor, R. G. (2010). Framing Hazards in the Health Arena. In J. C. Banaszak-Holl, S. R. Levitsky and M. N. Zald (eds.), *Social Movements and the Transformation of American Health Care*. Oxford: Oxford University Press, 284–99.

Snow, D. (2013). Grievances, Individual and Mobilizing. In D. Snow, D. della Porta, B. Klandermans and D. McAdam (eds.), *Blackwell Encyclopedia on Social and Political Movements*. Oxford: Blackwell, 540–42.

Snow, D., Cress, D. M., Downey, L., and Jones, A. W. (1998). Disrupting the 'Quotidian': Reconceptualizing the Relationship between Breakdown and the Emergence of Collective Action. *Mobilization*, 3, 1–22.

Snowden, F. M. (2020). *Epidemics and Society.* New Haven: Yale University Press

Sobhi, M. (2020). From Communal Violence to Lockdown Hunger: Emergency Responses by Civil Society Networks in Delhi, India. *Interface: A Journal for and about Social Movements*, 21(1), 47–52.

Sousa Santos, B. (2020). La cruel pedagogía del virus. In B. Bringel and G. Pleyers (eds.), *Alerta Global*. Buenos Aires: Clacso, 35-40.

Spear, R., Erdi, G., Parker, M. A., and Anastasia, M. (2020). Innovations in Citizen Response to Crises: Volunteerism and Social Mobilization during COVID-19. *Interface: A Journal for and about Social Movements*, 21(1), 383–91.

Staggenborg, S. (1993) Critical Events and the Mobilization of the Pro-Choice Movement. *Research in Political Sociology*, 6, 319–45.

Starr, P. (2010). Dodging a Bullet: Democracy's Gains in Modern War. In E. Kier and R. Krebs (eds.), *In War's Wake*. Cambridge: Cambridge University Press, 50–66.

Tarrow, S. (1989). *Democracy and Disorder*. Oxford: Clarendon Press.

Tarrow, S. (2022). *Power in Movement*. Cambridge: Cambridge University Press.

Tarrow, S. (2015). *War, States and Contention*. Cambridge: Cambridge University Press

Tassinari, A., R. Chesta and L. Cini (2020). Labour Conflicts over Health and Safety in the Italian Covid-19 Crisis. *Interface: A Journal for and about Social Movements*, 12(1), 128–38.

Taylor, V., and Leitz, L. (2010). From Infanticide to Activism: Emotions and Identity in Self Help Movements. In J. C. Banaszak-Holl, S. R. Levitsky and M. N. Zald (eds.), *Social Movements and the Transformation of American Health Care*. Oxford: Oxford University Press, 266–83.

Taylor, V., and Zald, M. N. (2010). Conclusion: The Shape of Collective Action in the U.S. Health Sector. In J. C. Banaszak-Holl, S. R. Levitsky and M. N. Zald (eds.), *Social Movements and the Transformation of American Health Care*. Oxford: Oxford University Press, 300–18.

Teivainen, T., and Huotari, P. (2020). Gobernanza global y horizontes democráticos más allá del coronavirus. In B. Bringel and G. Pleyers (eds.), *Alerta Global*. Buenos Aires: Clacso, 41–8.

Therborn, G. (2013). *The Killing Fields of Inequality*. Cambridge: Polity

Thieme, S., and Tibet, E. (2020) New Political Upheavals and Women Alliances in Solidarity Beyond 'Lock Down' in Switzerland at Times of a Global Pandemic. *Interface: A Journal for and about Social Movements*, 21(1), 199–207.

Thierny, K. (2019). *Disasters*. Cambridge: Polity

Thompson. C. (2020). #FightEveryCrisis: Re-Framing the Climate Movement in Times of a Pandemic. *Interface: A Journal for and About Social Movements*, 21(1), 225–31.

Tilly, C. (1975). *The Formation of National States in Western Europe*. Princeton: Princeton University Press.

Tilly, C. (1978). *From Mobilization to Revolution*. Reading, MA: Addison-Wesley.

Tilly, C. (1992). Where do Rights Come From? In L. Mjoset (ed.), *Contributions to the Comparative Politics of Development*. Oslo: Institute for Social Research, 9–37.

Trenz, H. J., Heft, A., Vaughan, M., Pfetsch, B. (2020). *Resilience of Public Spheres in a Global Crisis*. Weizenbaum Series no. 11. Berlin: The German Internet Institute.

Trott. B. (2020). Queer Berlin and the Covid-19 Crisis: A Politics of Contact and Ethics of Care. *Interface: a Journal for and about Social Movements*, 21(1), 88–108.

Turner, B. S. (2021). The Political Theology of Covid-19: A Comparative History of Human Responses to Catastrophes. In G. Delanty (ed.), *Pandemics, Politics and Society*. Berlin: De Gruyter, 139–56.

Turner, R. (1996). The Moral Issue in Collective Action. *Mobilization*, 1, 1–15.

Turner, R., and Killian, L. (1987). *Collective Behavior*. Englewood Cliffs: Prentice Hall.

Turner, S. (2021). The Naked State: What the Breakdown of Normality Reveals. In G. Delanty (ed.), *Pandemics, Politics and Society*. Berlin: De Gruyter, 43–58.

URGENCI (2020). Community Supported Agriculture is a Safe and Resilient Alternative to Industrial Agriculture in the Time of Covid-19. *Interface: A Journal for and about Social Movements*, 21(1), 274–9.

Vandenberghe, F., and Véran, J. F. (2021). The Pandemic as a Global Social Total Fact. In G. Delanty (ed.), *Pandemics, Politics and Society*. Berlin: De Gruyter, 171–90.

Van Dyke, N., and McCammon, H. J. (2010). *Strategic Alliances: Coalition Building and Social Movements*. Minneapolis: University of Minnesota Press.

Ventura Alfaro, M. J. (2020). Feminist Solidarity Networks Have Multiplied Since the COVID-19 Outbreak in Mexico. *Interface: A Journal for and about Social Movements*, 21(1), 82–7.

Ypi, L. (2012). *Global Justice and Avant-Garde Political Agency*. Oxford: Oxford University Press.

Walby, S. (2021). Social Theory and COVID: Including Social Democracy. In G. Delanty (ed.), *Pandemics, Politics and Society*. Berlin: De Gruyter, 191–208.

White, J. (2020). *Politics of Last Resort*. Oxford: Oxford University Press.

White, J. (2021). Emergency Europe after Covid-19. In G. Delanty (ed.), *Pandemics, Politics and Society*, Berlin: De Gruyter, 75–92.

Widmaier, W. W., Blyth, M., & Seabrooke, L. (2007). Exogenous Shocks or Endogenous Constructions? The Meanings of Wars and Crises. *International Studies Quarterly*, 51(4), 747–59. https://doi.org/10.1111/j.1468-2478 .2007.00474.x.

Wood, L. (2020a). We're Not All in This Together. *Interface: A Journal for and about Social Movements*, 21(1), 34–8.

Woods, L. (2020b). Social Movements as Essential Services. *Open Movements – ISA 47 Open Democracy*. www.opendemocracy.net/en/demo craciaabierta/social-movements-essentialservices/.

Workers Inquiry Network (2020). *Struggle in a Pandemic: A Collection of Contributions on the COVID-19 Crisis*. Workers Inquiry Network, Creative Commons Licence. www.intotheblackbox.com/wp-content/uploads/2020/ 05/Struggle-in-a-Pandemic-FINAL.pdf.

Zeller, M. (2020). Karlsruhe's 'Giving Fences': Mobilization for the Needy in Times of COVID-19. *Interface: A Journal for and about Social Movements*, 21(1), 292–303.

Zhang, J. (2020). Implicaciones de la censura en China durante la crisis de la COVID-19. In B. Bringel and G. Pleyers (eds.), *Alerta Global*. Buenos Aires: Clacso, 49–56.

Zielonka, J. (2021). Who Should Be in Charge of Pandemics? Scientists or Politicians? In G. Delanty (ed.), *Pandemics, Politics and Society*. Berlin: De Gruyter, 59–74.

Acknowledgments

I wish to thank my colleagues at the Center on Social Movement Studies (Cosmos) at the Scuola Normale Superiore in Florence at the Center for Civil Society Research at the Social Science Center in Berlin as well as David Meyer and Suzanne Staggenborg for very helpful suggestions. I am also grateful to the Alexander von Humboldt Foundation for awarding me a Research Prize and to Emmet Marron for having improved my English.

Cambridge Elements

Contentious Politics

David S. Meyer
University of California, Irvine

David S. Meyer is Professor of Sociology and Political Science at the University of California, Irvine. He has written extensively on social movements and public policy, mostly in the United States, and is a winner of the John D. McCarthy Award for Lifetime Achievement in the Scholarship of Social Movements and Collective Behavior.

Suzanne Staggenborg
University of Pittsburgh

Suzanne Staggenborg is Professor of Sociology at the University of Pittsburgh. She has studied organizational and political dynamics in a variety of social movements, including the women's movement and the environmental movement, and is a winner of the John D. McCarthy Award for Lifetime Achievement in the Scholarship of Social Movements and Collective Behavior.

About the Series

Cambridge Elements series in Contentious Politics provides an important opportunity to bridge research and communication about the politics of protest across disciplines and between the academy and a broader public. Our focus is on political engagement, disruption, and collective action that extends beyond the boundaries of conventional institutional politics. Social movements, revolutionary campaigns, organized reform efforts, and more or less spontaneous uprisings are the important and interesting developments that animate contemporary politics; we welcome studies and analyses that promote better understanding and dialogue.

Cambridge Elements ⹀

Contentious Politics

Printed in the United States
by Baker & Taylor Publisher Services